The RHS Encyclopedia of Practical Gardening

GROWING VEGETABLES

—————————— TONY BIGGS ——————————

Editor-in-chief Christopher Brickell

Technical Editor Kenneth A. Beckett

Tony Biggs has for many years been closely involved
in horticulture education, both in Britain and Australia.

MITCHELL BEAZLEY

The Royal Horticultural Society: Growing Vegetables
by Tony Biggs

The Royal Horticultural Society's Encyclopedia of
Practical Gardening
Copyright © Octopus Publishing Group Ltd 1979, 1992, 1999

The Royal Horticultural Society's Encyclopedia of
Practical Gardening: Growing Vegetables
Copyright © Octopus Publishing Group Ltd 1979, 1992, 1999

First published as The Royal Horticultural Society's
Encyclopedia of Practical Gardening: Vegetables
Copyright © Octopus Publishing Group Ltd 1999

First published in Great Britain in 1979
by Mitchell Beazley, an imprint of
Octopus Publishing Group Ltd,
2–4 Heron Quays, London E 14 4JP
An Hachette Livre Company
www.octopusbooks.co.uk

First published 1979
Second edition 1992

Reprinted 1993, 1994, 1995, 1996, 1997, 1998
This edition 1999
Reprinted 2000, 2001, 2002 (twice), 2003, 2004, 2005, 2006
(three times), 2007, 2008, 2009

The publishers will be grateful for any information that will assist
them in keeping future editions up to date. Although all reasonable
care has been taken in the preparation of this book, neither the
publishers nor the author can accept any liability for any
consequence arising from the use thereof, or the information
contained therein.

ISBN: 978 1 84000 152 5

A CIP record for this book is available from the British Library

Produced in Hong Kong by Toppan Printing Company Ltd
Printed and bound in Hong Kong by Toppan Printing Company Ltd

Contents

Introduction

The rewards of vegetable gardening have been justifiably proclaimed many times before. Ecologists, gourmets, health enthusiasts and consumer conscious people agree that growing vegetables is a worthwhile pursuit; it can also be extremely enjoyable. This book has been written and designed to ensure that, in addition, it is a successful one. *Vegetables* assumes no prior knowledge and cuts no corners; it reveals what the experts do and, also, why they do it.

Flavour and freshness
A major incentive for the home grower must be the vastly superior flavour of fresh vegetables that have been personally selected and tended. Understandably enough, the commercial grower is principally concerned with high yields, uniformity of appearance, the ability of a vegetable to be stored or transported long distances and remain in an acceptable condition, and other marketing factors. Varieties are selected to meet these requirements and, unfortunately, flavour often has to be a lesser consideration.

The home grower need not be so restricted and varieties can be chosen to suit personal tastes.

The benefits of science
The advances made in commercial growing over the past 25 years have not, however, been ignored in this book. *Vegetables* has an unashamedly scientific approach. This has not meant a rejection of the accumulated wisdom of practical vegetable gardeners; but such experience has been reinforced, and only occasionally modified, in the light of modern research.

Over the last two decades tremendous strides have been made in the development of highly efficient systems of commercial vegetable production, which can be of value to home gardeners. An understanding of how plants grow and respond to various conditions and techniques can increase the satisfaction and profit to be gained from tending a vegetable plot. In this connection the work of Horticulture Research International at Wellesbourne in Warwickshire has been gratefully incorporated. The plant spacings recommended throughout the book and the introductory sections on watering and sowing are influenced by HRI research.

Climate and local conditions
Despite the helpful conclusions of modern research and the step-by-step approach, the successful vegetable gardener must also be sensitive to and be able to interpret local conditions. *Vegetables* has been written for growers who live in cool temperate climates and, where possible, the range of climatic variations within this category has been accommodated. Sowings can take place earlier in a mild and favourable location such as the south of England than they can in the north, for example. The section on cloches and cold frames demonstrates how plants can be protected against adverse climatic conditions.

Again, bird damage is something which many gardeners will never have to contend with as it depends to a large extent on the incidence of particular bird populations. In each situation the grower must be ready to take action according to an informed interpretation of local conditions. It is always a good idea to talk to other local gardeners to find out what does well.

Pests and diseases
Throughout *Vegetables* great emphasis has been laid on the importance of preventative gardening. Factors such as thinning, watering and the selection of varieties are stressed as the keys to healthy vegetable production. However, the causes, symptoms and control of common pests and diseases are mentioned under each vegetable. An introductory section provides more information about the chemicals involved, their methods of application and the operations suggested throughout the book. **Remember to keep all chemicals out of the reach of children; label the containers carefully; and always follow the manufacturer's instructions.**

The gardener whose plants are plagued by pests and diseases should refer to *Garden Pests and Diseases*, a companion volume in this series.

Glossary

Aeration The incorporation of air into the soil.

Annual A plant that completes its life-cycle within one season.

Bare-root plant A plant lifted from the open ground with very little soil around the roots (as opposed to a pot-grown plant).

Base dressing Fertilizer applied immediately before sowing or planting.

Biennial A plant that completes its life-cycle over two seasons.

Blanching The exclusion of light from a plant to whiten the stems, shoots or leaves.

Bolting Premature flowering or "running to seed".

Brassica The cabbage, cauliflower and turnip genus of the Cruciferae.

Broadcast sowing A uniform distribution of seed over an entire seedbed, as opposed to sowing in a drill.

Calyx The outer whorl of a flower, consisting of sepals which may be free to the base or partially joined, as in tomato flowers.

Cap A hard crust on the soil surface.

Catch crop A rapidly-maturing crop grown between harvesting one vegetable and sowing or planting the next on the same ground.

Chard The young stems of salsify, seakale beet or globe artichokes.

Chicon The large, swollen white bud produced from forced chicory roots.

Chitting The germination or sprouting of seed prior to sowing.

Compost (garden) Rotted organic matter used as an addition to or substitute for manure.

Compost (seed and potting) Commercial peat or loam-based mixture with added fertilizers used for seedlings or pot-grown plants.

Compound fertilizer One which contains all three major constituents needed for healthy growth, ie nitrogen, phosphorus and potassium.

Crown The part of a plant at or close to ground level that normally produces stems: also the whole rootstock, especially when it is planted to produce a crop such as rhubarb.

Cultivar see Variety.

Cutting A separated piece of stem, root, or leaf taken in order to propagate a new plant.

Dibber A tool that is pushed into the soil to make a hole in which to plant a seedling, cutting or small plant.

Dormant Asleep. A dormant seed or plant is one that is in a temporary resting state during adverse climatic conditions.

Earthing up Mounding earth around the base and stems of a plant.

Eye A bud.

Fertilizer Material that provides plant food. It can be organic, ie derived from decayed plant or animal matter, or inorganic, ie made from chemicals.

F_1 hybrid A plant that is the result of a cross between two parent strains, usually with the best features of each. It does not breed true in further generations.

Foliar feed A solution of plant nutrients sprayed on to the leaves.

Forcing The hastening of growth by providing warmth and/or excluding light.

Friable Describes a fine and crumbly soil with no hard or wet lumps.

Frost-lifting The loosening and lifting of plants in the soil after hard frost.

Fungicide A chemical that kills fungi.

Genus (plural genera) A group of allied species in botanical and zoological classifications.

Germination The sprouting of seeds.

Growing point The extreme tip of roots or shoots. Shoots are sometimes removed to encourage growth. See Pinching out.

Growing season The period from planting to maturity of a particular crop during one season. Also, generally, the number of frost-free days per year in a given area.

Half-hardy A plant unable to survive the winter without protection.

Harden off To acclimatize gradually plants grown under glass to colder conditions outside; usually done in a cold frame, by exposing the plants to more air daily.

Hardy A plant capable of surviving winter conditions in the open without protection.

Heel cutting see page 176.

Heeling in The storing of plant material, upright or inclined, in a trench which is then filled in with soil and firmed.

Herbicide A chemical used to kill or control weeds.

Humus Fertile, decomposed organic matter in the soil.

Hybrid A plant produced by the cross fertilization of two species or variants of a species.

Inhibit To suppress a particular growth or developmental pattern.

Insecticides Substances used to kill injurious insects and some other pests.

Lateral A side growth that develops at an angle to the main axis. Lateral shoots are side-shoots which grow from lateral buds on a main or leading stem.

Legumes Vegetables of the family Leguminosae that produce pods, such as peas or beans.

Light The glass or plastic covering of a cold frame.

Manure Bulky material of animal origin added to soil to improve its structure and fertility.

Marble stage The stage when developing potato tubers are about the size of a marble, approximately ½ in in diameter.

Mature Capable of bearing flowers and reproduction.

Mulch A layer of soft material, such as straw, peat or compost, spread on the soil to conserve moisture and suppress weeds.

Mutant or sport A plant that differs genetically, usually in one characteristic, from the typical growth of the plant that produced it.

Offsets Small bulbs produced at the base of the parent bulb; also a young plant developing beside the parent from a runner.

Pan A hard layer beneath the soil surface.

Pelleted seeds Small seeds coated to make them easier to handle for space sowing.

Perennial A plant that lives for more than three seasons.

Pesticide A chemical used to kill or deter pests.

Pinching out, pinching or stopping The removal of the growing tip of a shoot to prevent further terminal growth and to encourage the production of side-shoots.

pH The degree of acidity or alkalinity. Below 7.0 on the pH scale is acid, above it is alkaline.

Pricking out The transplanting of a seedling from a seed tray to a pot or another tray.

Rhizome A lateral-growing, usually food-storing, stem that grows on or just hidden below the soil surface.

Root cuttings Pieces of root that are used to propagate new plants.

Rootstock The underground part of a plant from which roots and shoots are produced;

also the root system and stem on which a scion is grafted.

Seed leaves The first leaf or leaves produced by a germinated seed.

Sets Whole or part bulbs or tubers used for propagation.

Seedcoat The tough, protective layer around a seed.

Space sowing or station sowing The sowing of seeds individually at a set spacing in the site in which they will grow until pricking out or harvesting.

Spit depth The depth of a blade on a normal digging spade; about 10 in.

Sport *see* Mutant.

Stopping *see* Pinching out.

Strike To take root, usually of cuttings.

Sucker A secondary shoot that develops from a stem or root at or below ground level. Also a type of sap-feeding insect.

Systemic fungicide or insecticide A chemical which permeates a plant's sap stream and kills some diseases or sucking insects.

Thongs Cuttings from the roots of seakale.

Tilth The cultivated surface of the soil. Good tilth is fine and crumbly with no large stones or lumps of earth.

Tine The prong of a fork, hoe or rake.

Top dressing A fertilizer applied to established crops, usually more effective if hoed or watered into the surface of the soil.

Transpiration The loss of water through the leaves of plants as water vapour.

True leaves Leaves typical of the mature plant as opposed to the usually simpler seed leaves, which are the first to appear.

Truss The collective name for a group of flowers, such as those on tomatoes, that develop into fruit.

Tuber A swollen underground stem modified for food storage; the edible portion of plants such as potatoes.

Turgid Plant material that contains its full complement of water.

Variety A distinct variant of a species, either arising in cultivation (a cultivar) or occurring naturally.

Virus Disease-causing organism not visible to the naked eye, always transmitted by a vector, often an insect.

Wind-rock The loosening of a plant's root system by strong winds.

Tools

Always choose tools to match height and build and when buying a spade or fork, pick up several different types and go through the motions of digging to make certain that the balance and weight suit and that they are comfortable to use. A 30 in handle on a spade or fork is about right for the person of average height who likes to dig with a straight back; a 28 in handle often suits those who bend their backs slightly when digging.

Design and materials

Avoid flimsy, poorly made tools however cheap they may be. Badly designed tools made of materials that bend after a little use or with a rough finish or narrow spaces between the tines, where the soil clogs, are worthless. Conventional good quality steel tools with a smooth finish should be used to obtain the best results with the least physical effort. Stainless steel tools are durable and require only minor maintenance, but they are expensive and sometimes heavy and exhausting to use. If the weight and balance are suitable, however, they are undoubtedly the "best buy" because cleaning and oiling is minimal and they will last for many years.

Specially designed tools are available for the elderly and disabled, and some of these may be useful for gardeners who suffer from back trouble or who find that conventional tools do not suit them for some other reason.

Maintenance

Always clean garden tools and oil the metal parts as soon as possible after use. Store them in a dry shed or garage. This is not simply an aesthetic consideration because rusty tools mean harder work and they need replacement more quickly than tools cared for by washing, drying and rubbing over with an oily rag.

Mechanization

If a large area of land is to be used for vegetables, powered garden cultivators with rotating tines or blades that churn up the soil may save hand-digging. Their use is neither practical nor economical on small plots, however, because to use them efficiently for inter-row cultivation, widely spaced rows at least 30 ft long are required as well as sufficient room to turn the machine at each end of the plot. This wastes valuable growing space and ultimately reduces the crop-yield.

The illustrations show the basic tools needed for successful vegetable growing, although some gardeners may find other tools not illustrated here to be useful.

Spade (a) Good quality steel or stainless steel with a strong thin blade for digging.

Garden fork (b) Good quality steel or stainless steel with four well-spaced, rounded or angled prongs for breaking up soil. A flat-pronged fork (c) may also be useful for lifting root crops.

Dutch hoe (d) With its 4 in flat blade, the ideal tool for inter-row cultivation, loosening the soil and uprooting weeds.

Draw hoe (e) Valuable for taking out seed drills and earthing up crops such as potatoes and celery.

Onion hoe (f) With a 3 in wide blade good for inter-row cultivation, particularly at the seedling stage.

Hand cultivator (g) With three (or sometimes five) tines, useful for inter-row cultivation to loosen the soil and dislodge weeds.

Rake (h) Essential for seedbed preparation, the rake's head is also useful as a measuring device for the 12 in distance between certain crop rows.

Trowel (i) With a short handle for planting out seedings.

Hand-fork (j) Useful for inter-row cultivation.

Watering can (k) Made of strong galvanized steel with a fine brass rose (l) with screw fittings. Strong plastic cans, if well-balanced when full, are as good. Avoid push-on roses because these may become loose and fall off when a full can is tilted suddenly. A perforated dribble bar (m) is useful for accurately applying liquid fertilizers or weedkillers.

Dibber (n) With a steel point to make holes for seedlings and deep-sown seeds. An old spade or fork handle, suitably tapered at the end, is equally good.

Garden line (o) On a strong reel for accurate and symmetrical row alignment.

Wheelbarrow (p) A strongly constructed and manoeuvrable barrow, either of wood or galvanized steel, with a pneumatic or hard rubber tyre. When full it should be well balanced and easily pushed.

TOOLS

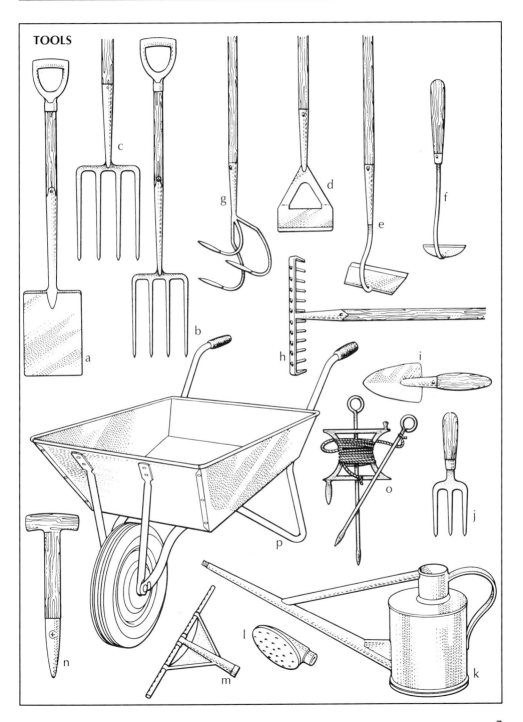

Preparing the ground 1

Not always the most popular chore in the gardener's calendar, digging is done for three reasons: to ensure that annual weeds are buried; to introduce manure or compost into the ground; and to aerate the soil. Fortunately this is only a once-a-year task, best tackled in autumn or early winter, leaving rough soil exposed to be broken down by the winter frosts. By the spring, soil that has been well dug should merely need superficial attention – raking or a light touch with the fork – in readiness for sowing or planting.

Properly carried out, digging should not be an unduly strenuous exercise. Once a good working rhythm has been established, digging a raw patch should be an enjoyable experience. Exhausted diggers are usually those who rush into the garden and proceed to attack their unruly earth without regard for some simple guidelines. Start off gradually and do a little at a time – half an hour the first day to get accustomed to the exercise should be sufficient. When the feel of the spade has been gauged, digging efficiently without too much physical effort becomes easier. Digging is a skill but it does not take long to learn and once acquired it gives the satisfaction of a well-prepared vegetable plot as well as the mastery of a new skill. As indicated on page 6, the choice of tools is also important, so be careful to select a spade and fork to suit your height. Remember that good quality steel tools are perfectly adequate and the more expensive stainless steel tools will not in themselves improve the digging. In preparing the ground, the garden line also comes into its own because the very first task is to stretch the line down the middle of the plot to divide it into two.

Single digging and double digging

As a rule it is sufficient to dig to a spade's depth (known as a spit deep). However, double digging may sometimes be required – for example to enrich deeper beds for permanent plants or to enhance the drainage of heavy soils. Either way, whether single or double digging, on cultivated soils or grassland, there are simple techniques to be followed to guarantee the best results.

The most efficient way of digging over soil is by the use of the trench method. This involves working across the plot in orderly trenches, each about 12-15 in wide or a spade's width, and then back-filling with soil. This way, only the soil heaped on the surface – that removed from the first trench dug – is used to fill in the final trench.

Working across the plot in this way, manure or compost can be introduced simultaneously as each successive trench is filled in. This should be done by spreading the manure on the surface first, if it is to be mixed in well. Otherwise the manure can end up in a lump at the bottom of each trench. Always check the requirements of each intended crop before doing this, however, as for some (such as carrots and parsnips) the incorporation of manure or compost is not beneficial.

If the ground requires an application of lime, this should never be dug in. Instead, lime is scattered on the surface, to be washed into the soil by rain. Lime should never be applied to ground freshly dug with manure, because the chemical constituents of the two tend to react with each other.

The key to successful digging is to keep the spade vertical. A slanting thrust, which achieves less depth, merely means that the work takes longer. Also, it is good technique to drive the spade in at right angles across the trench to free the clod of earth to be moved, enabling it to be lifted away cleanly.

The practice of growing vegetable crops without digging at all is often advocated. Adherents of the organic school of non-digging simply sow and plant on compost that has been laid over the surface of the soil. Underlying this practice – and it is a perfectly feasible one – is the theory of primeval forest regeneration in which bacteria work to convert layers of decaying matter into humus. Non-diggers argue that, while digging does indeed bury weeds, it also has the effect of reactivating weed seeds that have been lying dormant in the soil.

The non-digging method is technically a viable one: considerable fertility develops in the soil over a period of years and vegetables will grow successfully. The labour saved in digging must be offset by the cost of the compost, however, and experimental work has proved that the yield and quality of vegetables from dug plots is far superior.

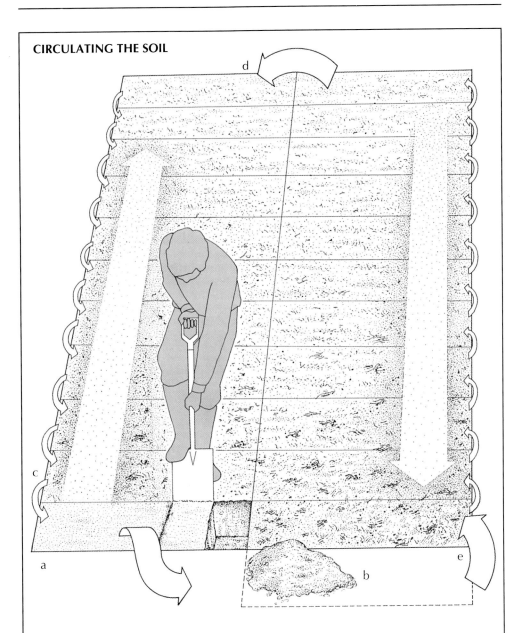

CIRCULATING THE SOIL

The plot is divided down the middle. Excavated soil from the first trench (a) is placed at the same end of the plot opposite the other half (b). The first trench is filled with soil from the second trench (c) and so on. The soil from the first trench in the second half fills in the last trench in the first half (d) and the last trench in the second half takes the soil removed from the first trench (e).

Preparing the ground 2

Single digging

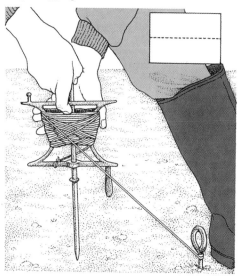

1 Autumn or early winter. Divide the plot down the middle with a garden line.

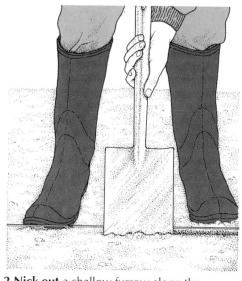

2 Nick out a shallow furrow along the division's length and remove the line.

5 Put the excavated soil in a heap at the same end of the plot opposite the other half.

6 Dig at right angles to slice off the next spadeful of soil, and repeat the process.

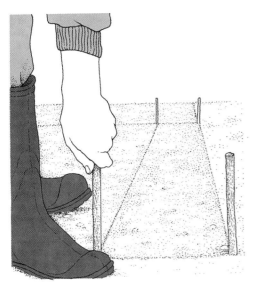

3 Mark a 12 in wide trench area at the end of one half of the pot.

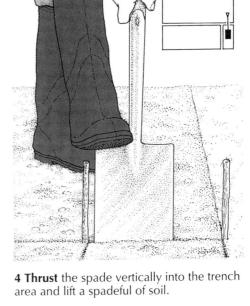

4 Thrust the spade vertically into the trench area and lift a spadeful of soil.

7 Incorporate manure or well-rotted compost if desired by digging it into the bottom of each trench before it is filled in with the excavated soil. Check the requirements of the crop before manuring.

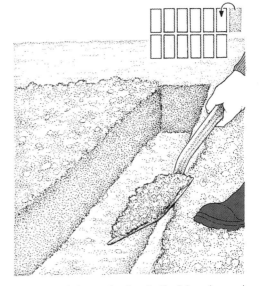

8 Proceed down the first half of the plot and fill the last trench with the soil removed from the first trench at the same end of the second half of the plot. This procedure should leave the plot level.

Preparing the ground 3

Double digging

Double digging, sometimes known as "bastard trenching", is an extra thorough way of preparing the ground. Because it improves drainage, double digging is an especially valuable exercise on heavy soils which may be waterlogged. Root crops, such as carrots and parsnips, grow deep into the ground in search of nutrients and water and if they encounter a hard "pan" or layer of soil beneath a spit's depth their growth is arrested. Such a hard pan may develop as a result of single digging over a number of years; compacted ground is a poor growing medium in any case and double digging may be the answer. Divide the plot down the middle and proceed around it as for single digging but take out trenches 24 in wide (instead of 12 in). Because the trenches are wider it is advisable to mark them out with sticks and a garden line. Dig the first trench to a spade's depth. Then loosen up the sub-soil at the bottom of the trench with a garden fork. The fork will penetrate a further spit of soil because its depth is about the same as that of the spade. Break up the soil all around the trench and not just the area in the middle. If incorporating manure, dig it into the broken-up sub-soil.

Double digging grassland

If the plot is a grass-covered area that has not been cultivated for some time, tame it for vegetable growing by adopting a different digging strategy. Divide the plot down the middle with a garden line. Nick out a shallow furrow along the division's length and remove the line. Mark out the first 24 in wide trench. First of all, skim off 2 in of turf with the spade and place it, with the right side up, opposite the other half of the plot at the same end (as with excavated soil in single digging). Dig the exposed soil to a spade's depth and place it in a separate heap near the sliced off turf. Then break up the sub-soil to a 12 in depth.

Chop up the skimmed off turf from the second trench and place it with the grassy part downwards, on top of the loosened up soil in the first trench; the excavated soil is placed on top, and so on. The turf sliced off the first trench is used to fill in the last trench.

If manure or compost is to be applied to grassland, mix it up with the broken-up soil before filling in with the chopped turves.

Double digging

1 Autumn or early winter. Mark out the first 24 in trench with a garden line and dig it to a spade's depth, placing the excavated soil at the same end of the plot but opposite the other half.

Double digging grassland

1 Skim off 2 in of turf from the first 24 in trench. Place this turf, grassy side upwards, at the same end of the plot opposite the other half.

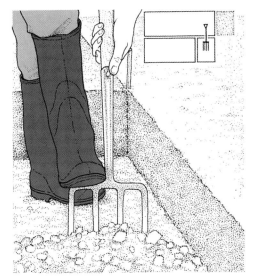

2 Fork up the sub-soil to a spit's depth and, if appropriate, in both grassland and cultivated plots, fork well-rotted compost or manure into the broken-up soil.

3 Fill in the first trench of a cultivated plot with the soil removed from the second trench. Repeat the operation until the plot is dug completely.

2 Dig the exposed soil to a spade's depth, placing the excavated soil in a separate heap near the removed turf.

3 Fill in the first trench with the turf sliced off the second trench by placing it, grassy side downwards, on top of the loosened soil and chopping it up. Place the excavated soil on top of this, and so on.

Watering

Vegetables depend on water in the soil to absorb the nutrients required for growth, and if insufficient water is available they cannot manufacture food. Water is also constantly lost through the leaves by transpiration and once the amount of water lost exceeds the amount taken in by the roots, wilting with a consequent reduction in growth and yield results.

Water also evaporates from the soil surface around plants and in temperate climates the total loss for leafy crops may be as much as 1 gal per square yard on a sunny day. It is obvious, therefore, that an adequate supply of water is essential to obtain the best growth, quality and yield possible. However, this does not mean drenching them every day, because an excess of water may well discourage root and shoot growth by inhibiting soil aeration and leaching away nutrients. It may also affect flavour adversely.

Seeds and transplanted seedlings require plenty of water to aid germination and growth but research has shown that the need for water varies markedly with different vegetable crops. Leafy crops, such as cabbages and cauliflowers, in which the foliage or shoots are eaten, benefit from frequent, regular supplies of water from the seedling stage onwards, provided that adequate nutrients are available. An application of 2-3 gal of water per square yard each week in dry periods during the growing season produces the best growth and yield.

In pod-producing vegetables, such as peas and some beans, too much water during the early life of the plants increases leafy growth at the expense of flowers and fruit. No artificial watering is necessary after the seedling stage (except in a drought), but give 1-2 gal of water per square yard weekly (or even twice weekly), at flowering time and as the pods develop to improve crops.

The timing of additional applications of water to certain vegetables is critical and will be described under the crop concerned. Always try to water crops in the evening or early morning when evaporation by the sun is low and apply it in reasonable quantities so that it penetrates deeply into the soil around the roots. Sprinkling water on the soil surface merely results in much of the water evaporating without reaching the roots where it is needed. Watering in the evening sometimes favours the spread of disease if the foliage remains wet overnight.

To avoid the need for constant watering of the vegetable plot it is important to make sure the soil is able to provide adequate supplies of water. On soils that do not retain

Water loss

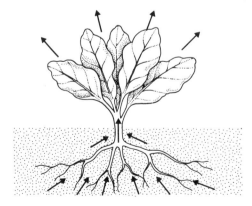

The plant's roots absorb water which passes up the stem and into the leaves. The water is then lost by the plant through its leaves by a process called transpiration.

Mulching

Reduce water loss by mulching the crop with well-rotted compost immediately after rain or artificial watering as soon as the plants are established.

moisture naturally, deep digging increases the volume of soil for the roots of the crops to penetrate in search of moisture. But the maximum benefit comes from regular applications of organic matter such as manure, compost, leaf-mould or moist peat. This should be thoroughly mixed into the soil as the plot is dug, not merely placed in a lump at the bottom of a trench.

Competition between the roots of neighbouring plants is another factor affecting water uptake. Weed competition should be eliminated at a very early stage and the distance between crop rows and the spacing of individual plants in the rows should be based partly on the water required by the crop concerned. Experimental work has provided information on the best spacing distances for various vegetables and these are given for each crop described.

Mulching crops with compost or leaf-mould is useful in cutting down water loss from the soil surface and it also provides a certain amount of additional food for the plants. The organic material used for mulching should be applied after rainfall or artifical watering as soon as the young plants have become well established. Cultivate the soil surface before mulching so that it is not too compacted. Mulching helps to suppress weeds and any weeds that develop on the mulch from windblown seed are easily pulled out of the loose surface.

Seeds require adequate water to germinate and, preferably, they should be sown when the soil is naturally moist. If the soil is dry, artificial watering is necessary. The whole area may be watered thoroughly a day or two before preparing the seedbed so that a good tilth can be obtained and the soil is sufficiently moist for germination to occur. Alternatively, water can be dribbled into the seed drill before sowing at a rate of about 1 gal to 20-25 ft length of the drill. Both methods are preferable to watering after sowing which in some soils "caps" the soil surface so that seedlings may have difficulty in pushing their way through.

Seedlings transplanted to their permanent positions require frequent watering. Each seedling needs approximately 1/4pt of water daily until it becomes re-established and it is better to apply the water around the base of the seedling than to spread it generally over the soil surface. In large areas this is not practical and a thorough daily soaking from a sprinkler is needed; although wasteful of water it does save time. In sunny weather seedlings may be covered with paper to reduce water loss.

Watering transplanted seedlings

Use a coarse rose on the watering can to apply 1/4pt of water around the base of transplanted seedlings daily in the morning or evening, until they are re-established.

Protecting transplanted seedlings

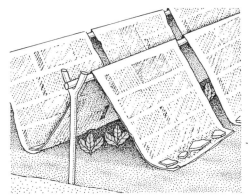

Cover transplanted seedlings with newspaper on sunny days to cut down water loss from the plants and soil. Replace the newspaper each morning if necessary.

Manure and compost

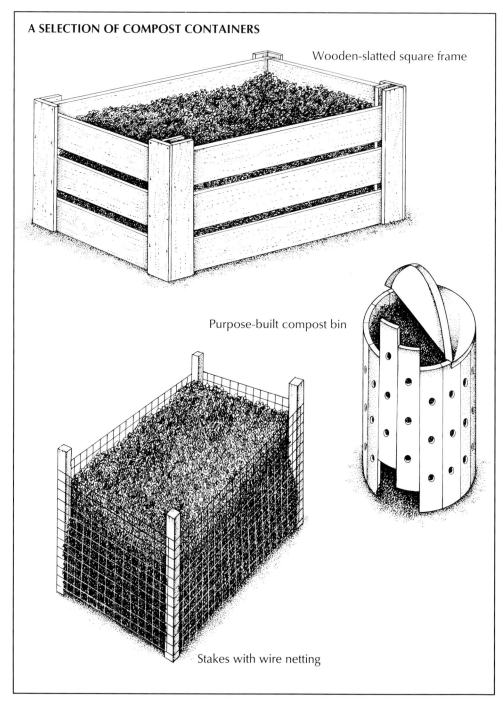

A SELECTION OF COMPOST CONTAINERS

Wooden-slatted square frame

Purpose-built compost bin

Stakes with wire netting

The fertility of a vegetable garden can be compared with a current bank account which is never allowed to become overdrawn. Growing vegetables every year quickly reduces soil fertility unless positive measures are taken to replace the losses. Manure and garden compost are used as soil conditioning agents. They maintain soil structure, provide the materials for bacterial action and improve the soil's moisture-holding capacity. They supply some of the nutrients required but usually not enough to maintain healthy growth, and so fertilizers (see below) are used to replenish the supply of plant nutrients in the soil.

Farmyard manure

Adding bulky organic manures helps to maintain fertility, although farmyard manure is a luxury which most gardeners have to do without today. If there is a local supply available take advantage of it, however, because well-made, well-rotted farmyard manure is still invaluable material with which to maintain a vegetable garden's fertility. Other locally available materials, such as spent mushroom compost or peat, can also help to condition the soil.

Garden compost

For most gardeners, however, good compost making is the key to fertility maintenance. Any healthy and uncontaminated green vegetation can be used to make compost. Never use woody material and avoid using vegetation which is seriously affected by pests and diseases, because some of these can survive the composting process. Similarly, plant material that has been sprayed with persistent, hormone weedkillers, such as brushwood killer, should not be used. Do not use brassicas affected by club-root, onions suffering from white rot, potato foliage affected by blight or potato roots from eelworm-attacked plants. This kind of unhealthy material is best disposed of along with household waste.

Building the compost heap

Build the heap directly on the soil. Waste materials are decomposed by bacteria which require air, moisture and nitrogen. Therefore the compost heap should be well aerated, moist (but not soaking wet) and of a size to allow heat to be generated and thus speed up the natural process of decomposition. A compost heap with a yard square base and a final height of 3-4 ft is very suitable. A pen of 1 in mesh wire netting, a purpose-built plastic compost bin or a wooden-slatted square frame keeps the heap tidy and less obtrusive in the garden. Without some such device to hold the heap together, birds can pull the sides to pieces.

Build up the heap in 6-9 in layers of waste vegetation. Do not use thick layers of any one material, such as grass cuttings, because this slows down the rotting process. Mix the materials well – the more they are mixed the better. When the first layer is finished and well packed, but not unduly compacted, apply a 1 in layer of garden soil and sprinkle this with lime if the soil is acid. Repeat the application after each subsequent 6-9 in layer. Garden soil supplies the soil bacteria which rapidly multiply and cause decomposition, and the lime keeps the heap sweet (see page 20). When the heap is completed cover the top with a thin layer of soil and cover this with old polythene sheeting to retain heat and encourage decomposition. The time taken before the composted material becomes friable and ready for use depends on the time of the year and the nature of the materials in the heap, but six months can be taken as a rough guide. A compost heap completed in October should be ready for use the following April. When green composting material is in short supply the soil layers can be sprinkled with ammonium sulphate or fresh manure to provide the nitrogen required, but never apply lime to the same layer as these activators.

Fertilizers

Short-term, major plant nutrient requirements are supplied by fertilizers. Nitrogen, phosphorus and potassium (NPK) are the main elements required by plants; calcium and magnesium are also of considerable importance. Sodium, iron, molybdenum, copper, boron, manganese and zinc are essential but only in small amounts.

Nitrogen fertilizers encourage vegetative

Manure and compost/Fertilizers

1 Select an area with a yard square base and start the heap with the first 6-9 in of vegetation. Mix the materials well.

2 Apply a 1 in layer of soil. Sprinkle each soil layer with lime if the soil is acid.

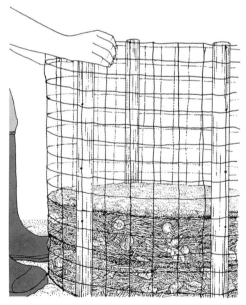

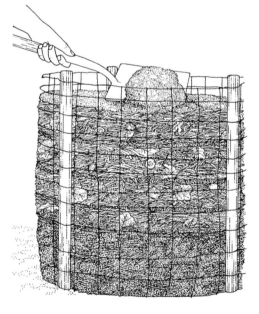

3 When the first 2 layers of vegetation have been prepared protect the heap with a circle of 1 in mesh wire netting.

4 When the heap is 3-4 ft high, cover it with a final 1 in layer of soil and then with polythene sheeting.

growth and are particularly important for leafy vegetables and for top dressing to promote rapid growth in the spring and summer. Phosphates are necessary for good root growth; they also encourage fruit ripening. Potash fertilizers balance the effects of nitrogenous materials and make the plant less soft, more cold-tolerant and more disease-resistant. The main effects of NPK are shown in the table below. Too much of one element may cancel the effects of others and the most important requirement is to provide a balanced mixture of the nutrients necessary for a particular crop.

Organic and inorganic fertilizers

Fertilizers may be organic or inorganic. Organic fertilizers are derived from animal or plant remains and include materials such as dried blood, meat and fish meal, and bonemeal. They tend to release their nutrients more slowly than do inorganic fertilizers, such as sulphate of ammonia, superphosphate of lime and sulphate of potash, which are produced by industrial processes.

Simple and compound fertilizers

Fertilizers may be simple or compound. Simple materials supply a major plant food only, for example, sulphate of ammonia supplies nitrogen, whereas compound fertilizers supply a mixture of plant foods. Growmore, for example, is a compound fertilizer which supplies balanced amounts of nitrogen, phosphorus and potassium. Compound fertilizers are generally used to provide the basic requirements of vegetables, and simple fertilizers – usually nitrogenous ones – are used to top-dress the plants.

Applying fertilizers

Crops normally receive most of their fertilizer requirements as a base dressing which is applied during the final soil preparations before the vegetables are planted or sown. For crops such as spring-sown onions, potatoes and the majority of root crops no more fertilizer applications are usually necessary. Other crops need further feeding, however, especially if rapid and continuing vegetative growth is needed over a long period. For

IMPORTANT PLANT FOODS

FOOD	EFFECTS	DEFICIENCY SYMPTOMS	MAIN FERTILIZERS
Nitrogen	Encourages leafy growth An excess delays flowering and fruiting An excess encourages soft growth which is easily damaged by cold and diseases	Stunted growth Pale yellow leaves Premature ripening, often with improved flavour	Sulphate of ammonia Nitro-chalk Calcium nitrate Nitrate of soda
Phosphorus	Necessary for good root development Encourages crop ripening Useful for strong seedling development	Poor, stunted growth Purple coloration of leaves and stems Poor seedling growth Fruits ripen very slowly	Superphosphate (placed close to the roots) Bonemeal
Potassium	Prevents soft growth Makes plants more winter hardy and disease-resistant Enables plants to withstand drought better	Generally slow growth High disease incidence Bronzing of leaves on some crops	Sulphate of potash Muriate of potash (more liable to cause damage to young plants)

Fertilizers/Garden lime

example, early summer cabbage should receive a balanced base dressing of a compound fertilizer such as a brand of Growmore but also benefits greatly from top dressings of nitrogenous materials such as nitro-chalk when in growth. With some crops, such as directly sown lettuce, there is a danger of putting too much nitrogenous fertilizer in as a base dressing because seed germination may be inhibited.

Base dressing crops
Base dressing fertilizers are applied during the final stages of soil preparation before sowing or planting. Rates of application usually range from 1-4 oz per square yard, and the material must be spread evenly. Divide the fertilizer into two lots and rake one lot up and down the area, and the other lot from side to side. This helps with even distribution. Very small quantities can be bulked up with soil, sand or sawdust to make distribution easier, but such materials must be thoroughly mixed in with the fertilizers.

Top-dressing crops
Top dressings are most commonly applied in solid form around the base of plants. Most fertilizers are formulated as fairly coarse granules but care is needed to ensure that they do not land in the middle of developing plants and cause burning and scorching of the young tissues. This is particularly important with nitrogen and potassium fertilizers. Phosphates, however, are best placed close to seeds or the roots of young plants. Always apply top dressings as close to the ground as possible and water the materials in immediately. This ensures that the top dressing has a rapid effect on plant growth.

Foliar feeding
A number of proprietary foliar feed materials are available, some of which are of organic origin. Foliar feeding is a convenient way of top-dressing plants but the effects are rarely as rapid and dramatic as using more conventional materials where the major elements of NPK are required. Foliar applications are very effective for correcting deficiency symptoms, however, particularly of magnesium and various minor elements.

Garden lime
Soils are derived from a wide variety of natural materials that may be alkaline (chalk or limestone soils) or acid (peaty soils) in reaction. An alkaline soil contains an abundance of calcium – an element required in small quantities by all plants. In very acid soils there is a shortage of calcium salts. The acidity or alkalinity of a soil is measured by the pH scale which ranges from 0 to 14. Chemically pure water has a pH value of 7, the neutral point. Acid soils have pH values lower than 7, and the pH value of alkaline soils exceeds 7. In Britain most soils tend to be slightly acid due to the constant leaching out of calcium by rain.

Equally important is the level of acidity or alkalinity best suited to various vegetable crops. It is obviously impractical to try to adjust the soil to provide the best level of acidity or alkalinity for each group, so a compromise is needed. Luckily, most vegetables grow well at a pH value between 6.0 and 7.0, and if the soil pH can be adjusted to and maintained at pH 6.0-6.5, even crops

Using a soil testing kit

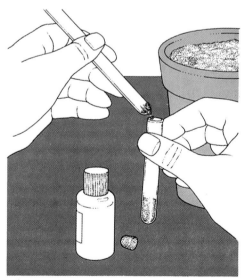

1 Take small, random samples of soil and mix them with the solution provided in the testing kit.

such as potatoes, which prefer a more acid soil, should thrive.

If the soil has a low pH the use of lime is advocated to neutralize the acidity if vegetables are to be grown. However, this cannot be achieved quickly and it may take a few years to obtain the desirable pH balance, particularly on light soils where there is leaching of nutrients by heavy rain.

The annual dressing of lime in autumn, regarded as obligatory by some gardeners, should never be given without first checking whether the soil is acid or alkaline.

Soil testing kits

The soil's pH level can be tested with one of the simple soil testing kits that are available from most garden centres. Take small random samples of the soil and shake them up with the solution provided in the kit. Allow the soil to settle and then compare the colour of the liquid with the range of colours on the chart also provided, which indicates the pH value by depth of colour. This can then be translated, according to the directions on the package, into the amount of lime needed.

Types of lime

It is always preferable to use ground limestone, which is safe and easy to apply. Other forms of lime (quicklime and hydrated, or slaked, lime) are available but they require careful application to avoid damaging plants in the vicinity. The rate of application varies from $1/2$-$1^1/_2$lb per square yard, depending on the pH, the soil, and the intended crops.

Applying garden lime

Apply lime in autumn or after winter digging so that the rains wash it in slowly. The best time for an application is a winter day when there is frost on the ground and therefore less chance of it blowing into the eyes. Seek a doctor's attention in the event of a mishap and always wash both face and hands immediately afterwards. Never use lime at the same time as manure, compost or fertilizers because lime may react chemically with these substances, thereby reducing their effectiveness.

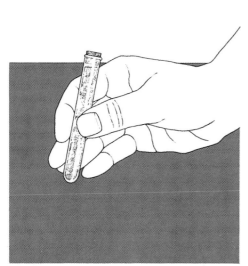

2 Shake the soil in the solution well and allow it to settle.

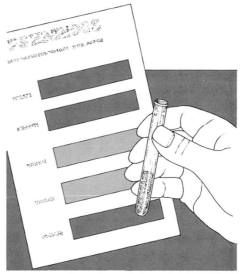

3 Compare the colour with the range of colours on the chart provided, which indicates the soil pH value.

Preparing a seedbed

After the ground has been dug in autumn or early winter the rough soil is exposed to the weathering effects of freezing, thawing and wetting (see pages 8-13). Drying spring winds then begin to break down the large clods of earth and form a friable crumb structure on the surface of the soil.

Preparing the tilth
A seedbed is prepared by cultivating this crumb structure to produce a tilth into which seeds can be sown or seedlings can be transplanted.

Cultivating First use a hand cultivator to work the top 6-8in of soil only, because it is important not to bring up large quantities of cloddy, unweathered soil, or buried weeds and organic manure from deep down. Cultivate thoroughly in both directions (ie at right angles to each other) to break down the surface clods and roughly level the surface. Do not over-work the soil at this stage because the tilth may become too fine for subsequent operations.

Applying fertilizer Base dressings of fertilizer are applied at this stage and any surface weeds or stones must be removed. Use a pronged cultivator to roughly incorporate fertilizer into the top 4-6 in of soil. Even application is important and where very small quantities are involved sand can be used to bulk it up, but it must be very well mixed.

Producing the final tilth
Traditionally any further consolidation of the soil required is by treading, shuffling the feet along or across the seedbed to break down the remaining lumps and fill depressions. However, this practice can seriously harm the soil structure, particularly that of a heavy soil. Whenever possible it is far better not to tread seedbeds but to use the head of a rake to break down any remaining clods, to firm any loose areas and to fill any depressions. On light "fluffy" soils treading may be necessary to produce a satisfactory seedbed. In these cases it is essential to tread very lightly and only when the soil is not wet so as to avoid damaging its structure.

Then use the rake with a rhythmic "forward-

Cultivating

1 February to March. With a hand cultivator cultivate the top 6-8 in of soil, using a "backwards-and-forwards" motion.

Consolidating

3 If necessary consolidate the soil by breaking up clods with the head of the rake and fill any depressions with soil.

Applying fertilizer

2 Roughly incorporate a base dressing of fertilizer into the top 4-6 in of soil and remove any surface weeds or stones.

Levelling

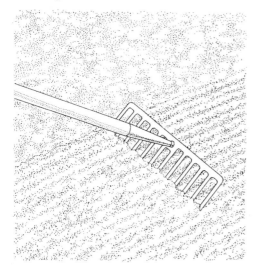

4 Rake to produce the final, level tilth. Move backwards and forwards with as little soil movement as possible, keeping the teeth of the rake only just in the soil surface.

and-backward" motion, and do not use it too deeply. If the initial cultivation has been done correctly it should not be necessary to move large quantities of soil.

The fineness of tilth

The type of soil and the kind of seed to be sown determine the fineness of tilth required. A finer tilth is needed for seed sowing than for transplanting and small seeds, such as lettuce, require a finer surface than do large seeds, such as peas and beans. Virtually any degree of fineness can be prepared on sandy or loamy soils, but silty and clayey soils must be treated much more carefully. Very fine silt or clay particles stick together in rainy conditions and then dry into a hard surface crust or cap through which it may be difficult for fine seedlings to penetrate.

Do not prepare very fine tilths on these kinds of soils. As a general rule it is best to prepare the coarsest sowing tilth that the particular seed tolerates, because the surface then remains more stable without "capping". This is particularly true for vegetables such as broad beans, which are sown in late summer or autumn for spring harvests.

Sowing vegetable seeds

Vegetable seeds can be sown directly outside or they can be transplanted after raising in a greenhouse or outdoor seedbed, or after purchasing from a nursery or garden centre.

Direct sowing Small seeds, such as those of lettuce and carrots, are usually sown in drills and subsequently thinned out to the required spacing. Always sow the seed very thinly in rows. Apart from saving seed, this cuts down competition for food between seedlings and it also produces sturdier plants. Mark out the position of the row with a peg at each end and stretch a garden line tightly between them. Use a draw hoe against the line to take out the drill, the depth of which should relate to the size of the seed – small seeds need shallow drills whereas larger ones can be sown deeper. After watering the bottom of the drill, the soil should be carefully raked back over the seeds and lightly tapped down with the back of the rake. Then label each row with the name and variety of the vegetable and the sowing date.

Sowing

Space sowing Large seeds, such as broad beans, runner beans and sweetcorn, can be space sown to their final spacings. Take out a drill as described above – obviously to a greater depth – or use a dibber or trowel to make a hole for each seed or group of seeds. It is impossible to be certain that each seed will germinate so it is better to sow two or three seeds at each station and thin out to one plant later if necessary.

Pelleted seed
Space sowing is a much more economical way of using large natural seeds but small seeds, such as those of lettuce, parsnip and carrot, can also be handled individually and space sown if pelleted seeds are used. These are seeds that are surrounded with a coat of clay-like material to facilitate more accurate sowing. Pelleted seed is expensive, however, and in some cases the results are unpredictable.

Pre-germinating or "chitting" seeds
Seed suppliers must provide a minimum percentage germination figure for dry, natural seed, but it is still impossible to know just how many will come up. Consequently, more seeds must be sown and then thinned out to produce the required number of plants and the right spacing. But it is possible to pregerminate, or chit, seeds before putting them in the ground. Then only those that have started to germinate are sown and seed can be used more economically. Pre-germination of seed can be carried out in a plastic container. It is a relatively easy task with large seeds but more care and skill is required when sowing small seeds.

Fluid drilling A technique known as fluid drilling has been devised at Horticulture Research International, Wellesbourne in Warwickshire. This allows pre-germinated seeds to be sown in a stream of fluid gel, such as fairly liquid wallpaper paste without fungicide, in a polythene bag from which the mixture of gel plus seeds is piped into the previously prepared and watered drill. The gel protects the germinating seeds.

Taking out a drill

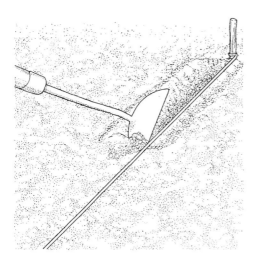

Direct sowing

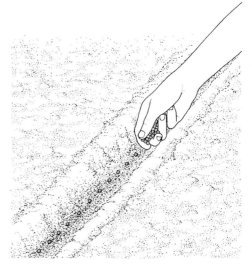

1 Stretch a garden line tightly between pegs at each end of the intended row. Keep the corner of the hoe tightly against the line to make a V-shaped drill.

2 Water the bottom of the drill. Allow the water to drain before sprinkling seeds very thinly and regularly along it. Then cover the seeds with soil.

Asparagus, established crowns
  20 bundles 1 lb per bundle
Beans, broad 44 lb
Beans, dwarf French 26½ lb
Beans, runner 55 lb
  climbing French 55 lb
Beetroot 35 lb
Broccoli, sprouting 20 lb
Brussels sprouts 22 lb

Cabbage 1 head per plant
Carrots, main crop 26½ lb
Cauliflower, all types 1 curd per plant
Celeriac 35 lb
Celery 1 lb per stick
Chicory 40 roots
Courgettes
  12-18 fruits per plant

PRE-GERMINATION OR CHITTING

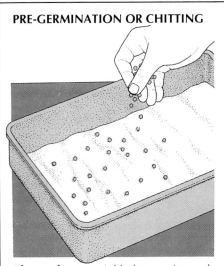

The seeds are sprinkled on moistened kitchen tissue in a container which is then covered and kept in a warm place (21°C/70°F) until they germinate.

Watering and thinning

Water is crucial for germination and it should be applied as a routine part of all seed sowing operations. Generous applications of water are particularly important for pelleted seeds because the clay-like material must be dissolved before the seed can emerge. In each seed sowing operation, however, in drills or holes and with natural, chitted or pelleted seeds, water the soil beforehand and keep the rows constantly moist until the seedlings emerge. Whenever possible water should be applied before sowing because watering seed drills after sowing can result in a "capped" soil surface which inhibits the growth of germinating seedlings. If this does happen keep the soil surface damp to soften the hard cap. Even thinly sown seeds produce more seedlings than will be needed and they must be thinned out. This is best done at the earliest possible stage because prolonged overcrowding encourages weak, leggy seedlings which are readily attacked by damping-off fungi. Remove unwanted seedlings carefully by hand and then water the rest.

Thinning

3 Remove unwanted seedlings as soon as possible, leaving the strongest plant at each station. Water the row of seedlings, and if necessary, firm afterwards.

Space sowing

Put 2-3 large or pelleted seeds at each position in the drill, then cover them and water. Later thin to 1 seedling per station if necessary.

25

Spacing/Purchasing seed

FLUID DRILLING

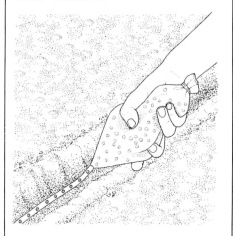

By this technique chitted seeds are piped from a polythene bag in a stream of fluid gel, such as a fairly liquid wallpaper paste without fungicide.

Transplanting

Always plant vegetables to a line and use a measuring rod to mark the correct in-the-row spacings. Plant with a dibber, a hand fork, or a trowel depending on the type of transplant being handled. Plants raised in pots, soil blocks or seed trays have quite large root systems and the holes are probably best made with a trowel. Make the holes large enough for the roots and plant at the same depth that they were in their container or seedbed. Dibbers can be used for transplanting leek and brassica plants raised in outdoor seedbeds because they have smaller root systems. On heavy, wet soils take care when using the dibber not to compress the soil at the sides of the hole because this can inhibit root spread and the establishment of transplants. It is also important to achieve the correct planting depth with a dibber and the soil must be firmed tightly around the plant roots of brassicas.

Water plants immediately after transplanting and again at regular intervals until they are established. Transplants are particularly liable to attack from birds.

The principles of spacing

Most of the spacings used in the home vegetable garden are used for traditional and historical reasons, but as new varieties are introduced (particularly F_1 hybrids) and requirements in vegetable size change, spacings may need to be reconsidered.

Plants develop most uniformly if the spacings between the rows are more or less the same as the spacings between plants in the row. This is not always practical, however, because a wider between-row spacing may be needed to allow for weed control, inter-row cultivations and access to other rows.

Growing plants closer together results in smaller plants in, for example, cabbage or cauliflower, but the plants also mature more evenly. This is also true of Brussels sprouts where close spacings result in smaller sprout buttons maturing evenly up the stems.

Close spacings put particular pressure on soil moisture and plant foods and if the soil dries out rapidly or has low reserves of organic matter they increase the likelihood of drought stress. Under these conditions – or if it is not possible to water the plants sufficiently regularly – it is better to place the plants farther apart and give the roots a larger volume of soil from which to draw their supplies of water.

Pest and disease spread is likely to be more rapid in closely spaced plants, and if rows of different vegetables are close together there is a danger of insecticide or fungicide spray drift on to adjoining rows.

Closely spaced plants exert a greater competitive effect against weeds, particularly if the crop plants have a spreading habit and can shade out the weeds. On the other hand, control of weeds may be more difficult in closely spaced plants because there is less space in which to use a hoe, and the danger of damaging the crops is increased.

Home vegetable gardens and allotments are generally highly productive areas of land. The range and quantity of vegetables produced from a small area is very great indeed and there are great pressures on the space available. The choice of crop spacings therefore depends on a careful consideration of all the factors in relation to the time and effort involved.

Endive 33 heads	Marrows 3-4 fruits (bush)	Potatoes, main crop 40 lb	Spinach beet 35 lb
Florence fennel 10 lb	6-8 fruits (trailing)	Radishes 25 lb	Sweetcorn 25 cobs
Globe artichokes	Onions, bulb 22 lb	Rhubarb, outdoor 35 lb	Tomatoes, outdoor
12-15 large heads	Parsnips 33 lb	Salsify 12½ lb	4-5 lb per plant
Kale 30-35 lb	Peas, early 15½ lb	Scorzonera 8 lb	Turnips 20 lb
Kohlrabi 20-30 lb	Peas, main crop 22 lb	Seakale 8-12 lb	
Leeks 40 lb	Potatoes, early 22 lb	Shallots 20 lb	
Lettuce 33 heads	Potatoes, second early 35 lb	Spinach 20 lb	

Purchasing seeds and plants

Planning the next season's cropping in the vegetable garden begins in the winter with the arrival of the new editions of seed catalogues. Many seed firms produce excellent catalogues which contain much valuable information.

Seed for the vegetable garden is relatively cheap and so it is worth while selecting and buying good quality seed. Buy from a reliable firm and use previous experience to choose varieties of proven performance. Be prepared to try something new but always grow a small quantity initially alongside the standard varieties. It is a good idea to consult other gardeners in the area to find out what does well in the locality. In Britain seed firms must, by law, state the purity and minimum germination percentages of their seed so there is a high degree of protection for the gardener.

F₁ hybrids

By a complex process in which two true-breeding plants are crossed to produce a hybrid generation (the first filial or F_1 generation), an increasing number of F_1 hybrids are appearing in the catalogues. The advantage of these hybrids is that they are often more vigorous than their parents, and they tend to have more uniform characteristics of height, form and colour, as well as maturing at the same time. F_1 hybrids are produced only after a considerable amount of selection and careful crossing over a number of years and they are invariably more expensive than conventional varieties. Never save seed from F_1 hybrids because the next generation of plants will have lost its uniformity.

F_1 hybrids do not suit everyone's vegetable requirements but they are ideal for those who want uniformly maturing produce to put into household freezers.

Conventional varieties

Conventional varieties mature over a longer period and they are preferred by many gardeners. One advantage is that seed can be saved from them, but it must be selected from healthy, true-to-type plants only.

Storing seeds

Seeds should be stored dry in paper bags or packets rather than polythene or plastic bags because these tend to conserve dampness if it is present. Store seeds in a cool, dry place, such as a cellar or a refrigerator, and keep all the packages clearly labelled.

If they have been stored correctly most vegetable seeds remain viable for at least two years. But because there are some exceptions – parsnip seed, for example, rapidly loses the ability to germinate once a packet has been opened – it is wise to buy several small-sized packets of seed.

Buying vegetable plants

Some vegetable plants are purchased from nurseries or garden centres. This is probably most convenient for tomatoes, cucumbers, sweet peppers, aubergines, celery and celeriac, but care is needed when purchases are made. Trust and goodwill between the nursery owner and the customer is essential so always return where good service has been received before.

Be certain of the varieties being purchased. In some situations it may be possible to ask nursery staff to raise plants of a favourite variety from seeds you provide.

Be very careful when buying plants that could introduce a persistent disease to the garden. This is particularly true for club-root on brassica plants and white rot on onion or leek plants, and the warning is even more applicable to plants which friendly gardening neighbours may provide.

With such acquisitions it is very important to know about the origins of the plants because it is almost impossible to eradicate disease once it spreads in the vegetable garden.

Buying perennial vegetables

Perennial vegetables such as rhubarb, globe artichokes and asparagus are purchased as plants rather than as seed. Again, they could be infected with virus diseases which gradually reduce the vigour and productivity of the plants, and so only virus-free or tested material should be purchased.

This is also true of "seed" potatoes which are likely to be bought every year. Virus-free seed tubers are produced in areas where aphids that spread viruses are not a problem.

Pests and diseases 1

Strong, healthy plants are less susceptible to disease and better able to withstand damage from pests. However, despite correct cultivation, vigilant weed control, crop rotation and the increasing availability of disease-resistant varieties, damage due to pests and diseases occurs even in the most carefully managed vegetable gardens. It is therefore important to be able to make a rapid and accurate diagnosis of each problem so that the right action, often involving the use of chemicals, can be taken as soon as possible.

The use of chemicals
Always follow the manufacturer's instructions precisely, especially concerning dilution, the time of application and the period which must elapse between the final application and harvesting. Always store chemicals, sealed and labelled, out of the reach of children, pets and wild animals. Never transfer them to soft drinks bottles. Do not spray on windy days and do not allow spray to drift on to other crops or neighbouring gardens, ponds, rivers, ditches or water sources. Never use containers previously used for weedkillers when mixing or applying other sprays and do not mix up more material than is required because it is difficult to dispose of the excess safely. Wash hands and equipment thoroughly after spraying.

The range of pesticides available to amateur gardeners for use on vegetables is very limited. None available for some problems, but *never* use pesticides which are not recommended.

Not all insects and animals in the garden are harmful to vegetables and some are beneficial. They can be killed by the chemicals used to control pests so never use pesticides indiscriminately or excessively.

Types of pesticides
Pesticides is a general term encompassing insecticides, fungicides, herbicides, miticides, molluscides, etc. Insecticides have different modes of action. Contact types such as derris affect the insect directly and it is important to cover all the plant's surfaces for maximum kill. They remain effective for a relatively short period after application. Systemic types such as heptenophos and

dimethoate are absorbed into the plant and spread through the sap. They are very effective against sap-sucking insects. Complete coverage of the plant is not essential. Most fungicides only check or prevent disease and should therefore be applied before signs of disease are seen. A few partially systemic fungicides such as carbendazim are now available. These are absorbed slightly into the plant's tissues and are effective for a short period even after disease symptoms are visible.

Methods of application Chemicals are available as dusts, sprays, pastes, pellets, wettable powders and aerosols. Not all chemicals are in all forms, however, and not all forms of a chemical are effective against the same range of pests or diseases.

Most chemicals are listed in this book according to their active ingredient and not by their trade name. Use products that contain the appropriate active ingredient which is given on the label or in the instructions issued by the manufacturer.

DISEASES
In the following section the main diseases are briefly described and appropriate control methods are recommended.

Blackleg of potatoes is caused by the bacterium *Erwinia carotovora* var. *atroseptica*. Early in the season the foliage of an affected plant turns yellow and the shoots collapse because of blackening and rotting of the stem bases, although occasionally one or two healthy stems develop. The plant may die before any tubers form but any which have already developed show a brown or grey slimy rot inside starting at the heel end. Destroy affected plants. If severely infected tubers are stored they will decay, but those only slightly infected may show no symptoms and, if planted, will introduce the infection the following season.

Chocolate spot disease causes discoloration on the leaves and stems of broad beans and can seriously affect over-wintered crops. Plants grown in acid soils or which have become soft through excessive applications of nitrogenous fertilizers are more susceptible to attack. Sowing the seeds thinly, applications of potash at $\frac{1}{2}$ oz per square yard before November sowing and the maintenance of a pH of 6.5-7.0 will cut down the likelihood of infection. Where the disease is endemic spray the young foliage with carbendazim before any symptoms are seen.

Club-root distorts the roots and badly affects the growth of all brassicas. Weeds in the brassica family are also attacked, eg shepherds purse. Crop rotations can prevent disease spread but club root is easily carried in soil, root debris and infected seedlings. The disease remains in the ground for many years but is more prevalent in acid soils, so where necessary raise the pH to 6.5-7.5 by applying ground chalk or limestone at 14 oz per square yard and maintain the pH level with smaller dressings as required in subsequent years. Seedlings may be dipped in a solution of thiophanate-methyl to protect them from attack.

Common scab of potatoes occurs most frequently in dry soils lacking in humus and is also prevalent on alkaline soils. A soil pH of 5.0-6.0 and improvement of the soil humus content will cut down the incidence of the disease. Potatoes should also be kept well watered, particularly during dry spells. No available chemical control measures are effective against it.

Damping off diseases of seedlings are encouraged by overcrowded, stagnant conditions and the use of garden soil rather than sterilized soils or compost for raising seedlings under glass. Affected seedlings rot and collapse at ground level. Thin sowing in sterilized compost will cut down the incidence of damping off. Slight attacks may be checked by watering with Cheshunt compound after removing dead seedlings.

Downy mildews may affect lettuce, onions, spinach and young brassicas. Thin sowing and early thinning of seedlings will cut down incidence of these mildews but if seedlings are attacked, remove the affected leaves and spray with mancozeb.

Foot and root rot is caused by several different fungi which kill the roots and bases of the stems of young plants. At the first signs of this disease, water the crop with a solution of Cheshunt compound. Mound sterile compost around the bases of affected tomatoes to encourage secondary roots up the stem. Destroy badly affected plants.

Grey mould (*Botrytis cinerea*) may affect most vegetables at some stage in their lives especially in humid weather. It is encouraged by overcrowded, stagnant conditions and affected stems, leaves or fruits rapidly rot and become covered with a grey-brown fungal growth. To cut down attacks sow seeds thinly in a seedling mix or compost rather than garden soil under glass. Keep seedlings and plants well spaced. Provide good ventilation under glass, making sure that air is taken in at a low level and rising through the leaves. Make sure that dead or dying material is removed and destroyed. During the growing season spray with carbendazim.

Halo blight is a seed-borne bacterial disease which appears as spots on the leaves of beans. The spots are surrounded by a light-coloured ring or halo. There is no adequate control and the plants should be burnt once the crop has been picked.

Leaf spot Brassicas, spinach beet and beetroot are among those crops susceptible to leaf spot fungi which usually affect older leaves, causing round brown spots. Sometimes affected tissues fall away, leaving holes. Leaf spot is most troublesome in wet seasons, particularly among overcrowded plants and on brassicas grown too soft as a result of heavy dressings of nitrogenous fertilizers. Affected leaves should be removed and destroyed. Proper thinning and crop rotation are important factors in the prevention of leaf spot infections.

Neck rot fungus (*Botrytis allii*) can cause considerable loss of stored onions. A grey mouldy growth develops on or near the neck of an affected bulb, which subsequently becomes soft and rotten. Later, large black resting bodies of the fungus develop on the rotting tissues. Store only hard, well dried bulbs in a cool, dry place where there is free circulation of air around them. A good method is an onion rope. Examine bulbs frequently and remove rotting onions as they are seen. The disease can be seed-borne, therefore buy good quality seed which has been treated against neck rot, or sets from a reputable grower.

Parsnip canker causes rotting of the shoulder

Pests and diseases 2

tissues of parsnips. There are no satisfactory control measures although the incidence of the disease can be reduced by growing parsnips on a fresh site each year in deep well-worked soil of pH 5.5-7.0. 'Avonresister' is a variety resistant to parsnip canker.

Potato blight is a serious disease of potatoes and is also liable to infect tomatoes. Foliage, stems and tubers of potatoes can be affected and destroyed. Deep planting of healthy tubers in drills at least 5 in deep and timely earthing up minimize infection. Main crop potatoes should also be sprayed from July onwards with mancozeb or bordeaux mixture to control the disease. Cut off and remove the haulms before lifting. A few varieties are resistant to potato blight and can be grown in areas where this disease is prevalent. Potato blight can be controlled on tomatoes by spraying each season with one of the chemicals recommended for potatoes, as soon as the tops have been pinched out of most of the plants in midsummer. In cool wet seasons the spray should be repeated every 2-3 weeks as a precaution.

Powdery mildews occur on marrows, outdoor cucumbers and some other vegetable crops, particularly if they become dry at the roots. The leaves and stems become covered with a white powdery coating. Control by spraying with carbendazim or dusting with sulphur as soon as the first symptoms appear, and repeat if necessary. Increase the frequency of watering.

Sclerotinia disease can attack the roots or stem bases of several vegetables including carrots, cucumbers, Jerusalem artichokes and roots or tubers in store. Any infected plants must be burnt to avoid further soil contamination from the last resting bodies that form if diseased plants are allowed to remain. There is no practical chemical control. Good hygiene and rotation of affected crops are the only practical methods of control.

Violet root rot of asparagus is caused by the soil-borne fungus, *Helicobasidium purpureum*, which kills the crown and roots. It grows on them as violet web-like strands. Small round masses of fungal threads may also appear. With the death of the roots the top growth turns yellow and dies, and a gap develops in the asparagus bed as the disease

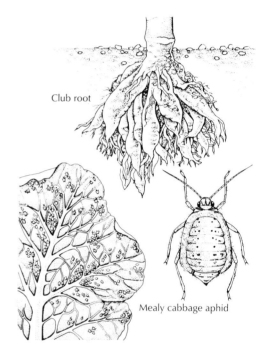

Club root

Mealy cabbage aphid

gradually spreads outwards. Where only slight infection has occurred, isolate the diseased area by sinking sheets of thick polythene into the soil to a depth of 12 in. In severe cases abandon the infected bed and make a new one on a fresh site.

Viruses causing leaf mottling and distortion and often stunting of the plants can affect marrows in particular, celery, cucumbers, tomatoes and several other vegetables. They are spread by aphids or eelworms and so control of these pests and removal of weeds that may act as hosts for both the viruses and their vectors is important. There is no cure for virus-affected plants, which should be destroyed once the trouble has been diagnosed. Always wash hands and tools after handling virus-infected plants to stop further spread.

White rot of onions appears as a fluffy white growth at the bases of onions and quickly affects and kills the foliage. Affected plants should be destroyed as soon as the disease is seen. Spraying with carbendazim to combat neck rot may give incidental control. White rot spores can remain in the ground for several years.

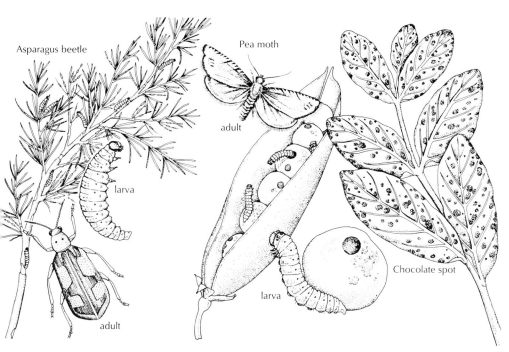

Asparagus beetle

Pea moth

adult

larva

larva

adult

Chocolate spot

PESTS

In the following section the main pests are briefly described and appropriate control methods are recommended.

Aphids (greenfly and blackfly) will infest most vegetable crops. Apart from the damage caused by the aphids themselves, they are carriers of virus diseases and vegetables should be checked regularly for their presence. Infestations should be dealt with at an early stage by spraying with dimethoate, derris, heptenophos, pyrethrum, or pirimicarb. If the plants are ready for harvest use derris. Cucurbits are also best sprayed with derris, pyrethrum or permethrin to avoid damage. Beans, if in flower, should be sprayed at dusk with pirimicarb because bees, the main pollinators, are relatively tolerant of it.

Root aphids may be troublesome on beans, lettuce and artichokes. Attacks are not usually noticed until the plants are infested. A heptenophos or pirimiphos-methyl drench may check infestations. Some lettuce varieties, such as 'Avoncrisp' and 'Avondefiance', are resistant to root aphids.

Asparagus beetle Small yellow, red and black beetles and their grey-black grubs can defoliate the plants during the summer. Control by spraying with derris, permethrin or pirimiphos-methyl as soon as these pests are seen outside the cropping season.

Bean seed fly maggots can prevent germination of French and runner bean seed and may also damage onions. Damage usually occurs in cold, wet seasons when germination is slow. The use of cloches to warm the soil early in the year encourages more rapid germination and cuts down attacks. Treating the seed row with pirimiphos-methyl or lindane dust gives some protection.

Birds Damage to vegetable crops by birds, mainly wood pigeons and sparrows, can occur throughout the year. Scaring devices and bird repellent sprays are of limited value in deterring birds. In some instances they may be effective for short periods, but where birds are a persistent problem some form of vegetable cage or netting is essential to produce worthwhile crops.

Cabbage root fly maggots can devastate brassica seedlings and young plants. The seed

Pests and diseases 3

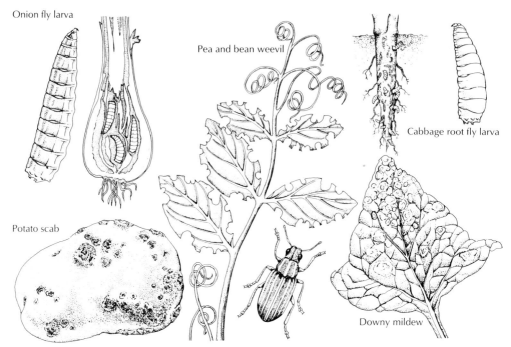

Onion fly larva

Pea and bean weevil

Cabbage root fly larva

Potato scab

Downy mildew

rows and transplanting sites should be treated with pirimiphos-methyl, lindane or chlorpyrifos prior to sowing or planting. Placing 6 in squares of carpet underlay on the soil around the stem base can protect transplants by preventing flies laying eggs in the soil. Attacks on established plants can be checked with a pirimiphos-methyl drench.

Carrot fly is the most damaging pest of carrots, parsley, parsnip and celery. Growth is stunted and secondary rots may develop in damaged carrots. Careful spacing of pelleted seed or very thin sowing to cut down the need to thin carrots will help to minimize damage as female carrot flies are attracted by the aroma of foliage bruised when thinning. Sowings made after May normally miss the first generation of maggots but carrot fly is such a widespread pest that treatment of the seed drills with lindane or pirimiphos-methyl is advisable. Carrots that are not to be lifted until autumn should also be sprayed with pirimiphos-methyl in early August. Some carrots, such as 'Sytan' and 'Fly Away' have some resistance to this pest.

Caterpillars are troublesome on cabbages and should be controlled before they penetrate the hearts, where they are difficult to reach. Hand picking with a small number of plants or treatment with bifenthrin, pyrethrum or permethrin is effective. Alternatively, control with a bacterial spray containing *Bacillus thuringiensis*.

Celery leaf miner lives in the leaves of celery, parsnip and lovage. Heavy attacks can be controlled by spraying with malathion. Light infestations of celery leaf miner can be overcome by hand-picking.

Cutworms are soil-dwelling caterpillars of various moth species. They feed on roots and the bases of stems and can attack most vegetables, especially lettuce, causing them to wilt and die. Control is by treating the soil with lindane or pirimiphos-methyl before sowing or planting crops.

Flea beetles Heavy infestations of these tiny beetles, which eat small holes in the leaves of brassica seedlings, can be controlled with derris, lindane, bifenthrin, or pirimiphos-methyl. Damage seldom occurs once the plants have developed beyond the seedling stage.

Glasshouse red spider mite is a common pest of all vegetables grown under glass, causing leaf discoloration and adversely affecting growth. A damp atmosphere helps to check this pest which thrives under hot dry conditions. Red spider mites often develop a resistance to pesticides. The best biological control is *Phytoseiulus persimilis*. Alternatively, spraying with bifenthrin, dimethoate or pirimiphos-methyl at seven-day intervals can control infestations. Care is needed when applying chemicals to cucumbers as they can be damaged. Spray in the evening when it is cooler and make sure that the plants are not dry at the roots.

Onion eelworm mainly attacks members of the onion family but can also damage carrots, parsnips and beans. They are microscopic, worm-like creatures that live inside the stem and leaves. They cause the tissues to become soft and swollen, and infested plants usually rot off and die. There are no chemical controls available to amateur gardeners and infested plants should be burnt. Host plants, which include some weeds, should not be grown in ground infested with onion eelworms for at least two years. Lettuce and brassicas are not attacked.

Onion fly attacks all members of the onion family. Young plants may be killed by the maggots, and the bulbs of older onions are tunnelled and made useless for consumption. Soil treatment with lindane or pirimiphos-methyl when sowing or planting will control this pest during the vulnerable early stages.

Pea moth caterpillars badly damage peas, eating the green peas and spoiling the crop, particularly of mid-season varieties. Early-maturing crops usually escape damage because they flower before the pea moth lays its eggs. Peas which flower between mid-June and mid-August should be sprayed with bifenthrin or pirimiphos-methyl 7-10 days after flowering starts.

Pea and bean weevils feed by eating notches from the leaf margins of pea and broad bean plants. Use lindane or pirimiphos-methyl dust only if seedlings are attacked.

Pea thrips (thunder flies) are tiny, thin, brown-black or yellow insects that suck sap from the leaves and the pods. This causes a silver-brown discoloration and damaged pods may be distorted and only partly filled with peas. Heavy infestations are more likely in hot, dry summers and damage can be prevented by spraying with dimethoate, pirimiphos-methyl or bifenthrin.

Potato cyst eelworms live in the roots of potato and tomato plants, and the foliage is often killed by midsummer. The yield is therefore much reduced. There are no chemicals available to amateurs that will control these eelworms. Crop rotation helps to reduce infestation but it may be necessary to stop growing potatoes on land badly affected by these pests. Some potato varieties are resistant to one species of eelworm (*Globodera rostochiensis*) and a few are tolerant of *G. pallida*.

Slugs, snails, woodlice and millipedes can destroy seedlings and attack many developing vegetable crops. Slugs can be controlled by using methiocarb or metaldehyde pellets along the rows. Methiocarb gives some control of woodlice and millipedes but where they are troublesome dusting the young plants with lindane may be necessary.

Whitefly Brassicas, cucurbits, tomatoes and other vegetables are attacked by various whitefly species that may cause a black deposit of sooty mould on the leaves. Cabbage whitefly is a distinct species from the glasshouse whitefly that affects tomatoes and cucurbits, but both may be controlled by three or four sprays with pyrethrum, permethrin, bifenthrin or pirimiphos-methyl at seven day intervals. Under glass, biological control with the wasp *Encarsia formosa* avoids the problems of pesticide residues and resistance.

Wireworms may occur in large numbers in grassland or weed infested areas. They attack the roots of many vegetables and may seriously affect the quality of potatoes. Soil dressings of lindane or pirimiphos-methyl dust at planting or sowing will control infestations.

Weed control

A weed is a plant growing where it is not wanted. Thus one of last year's potatoes which comes up in this year's carrots is a weed. Weeds compete with crops for light, water and nutrients and they also create a micro-environment around plants in which grey mould (*Botrytis cinerea*) and damping-off diseases flourish. Weeds also act as hosts for pests, such as aphids and whitefly, and diseases, such as club-root of brassicas.

Annual weeds and perennial weeds
Annuals are plants that complete their life-cycle within a growing season, and they are often able to undergo more than one life-cycle in a season. Annuals are also characterized by the production of very many seeds so that the weed seed population in the soil is constantly replenished. Perennial plants live from year to year and usually have underground organs – stems or roots - which enable them to survive through the winter. Thus docks (*Rumex* spp) have thick, fleshy tap roots and couch grass (*Agropyron repens*) has underground stems or rhizomes.

Controlling perennial weeds
Weed control beings with winter digging prior to growing the first crops. Cut down any woody perennials, such as brambles (*Rubus* spp), and dig out all the roots. Double dig the whole vegetable garden in the first instance and remove all perennial weed roots and rhizomes. Dispose of them all and never use them for compost making. Once the land has been cleared of perennial weeds, they should never be a problem again, unless, of course, they are imported with organic materials such as farmyard manure.

Controlling annual weeds
Annual weeds continually reappear, however, and all vegetable growing soils have a large reservoir of weed seeds. Weed seeds are also blown in on the wind and carried by birds and by man.

When winter digging, the gardener should skim off annual weeds and dig them into the bottom of each trench along with organic manure or garden compost. Digging brings up annual weed seeds which were buried in previous seasons. Many will germinate, but subsequent cultivations should kill the young weed seedlings that emerge. They will have appeared by the time cultivations take place to prepare the land for sowing or planting. Remove these, and the next flush of weed seedlings will appear with the sown or planted vegetables.

Hoeing against weeds
Hoeing is the main method of weed control

Hoeing

Carefully hoe annual weeds, keeping the blade level with the surface layers of the soil. Choose a warm, drying day for hoeing and keep the blade sharp.

Digging perennial weeds

During winter digging remove all perennial roots and rhizomes and burn them.

in the growing crop. It is largely a matter of personal preference which type of hoe to use, but in every case the blade must be kept constantly sharpened so that the weeds are severed from their roots rather than pulled up with them.

Choose a warm, drying day so that the weeds wilt and die quickly after hoeing. Care is needed when hoeing closely around crop plants because any damage caused is quickly colonized by disease organisms. Keep the hoe in the upper, surface layers of the soil so as not to bring up more weed seeds to germinate and cause further problems. The dry soil produced by surface hoeing acts as a mulch which in itself inhibits weed growth.

Mulching against weeds

Weeds can also be controlled by using mulches. The use of dry soil as a mulch has already been mentioned but materials such as black polythene, well-prepared compost, or peat can also be used. Black polythene forms a complete physical barrier to weed growth; it also warms up the soil and conserves moisture. It is usually necessary to bury the edges of the polythene to prevent it blowing away and holes must be cut in it through which vegetables can be planted or sown. As well as eliminating weeds, a black polythene mulch can bring crops forward and hasten

their maturity by as much as three weeks but, unfortunately, pests such as slugs can thrive in the moist conditions produced. Organic mulches, such as leaf-mould, perform similar functions but have the advantage that they can be dug into the soil at the end of the season, thus improving its structure and fertility. Straw is not recommended as a mulch material because the bacterial action required to break it down can lead to a nitrogen deficiency in certain soils.

Using chemicals against weeds

The amateur's vegetable garden is extremely productive and a large number of crops are grown in a very small area. The danger of spray drift and persistence from chemical weedkillers is therefore considerable. Against annual weeds the non-persistent contact weedkiller paraquat/diquat does have a place, however, but it must be applied at low level with a dribble bar when there is no wind and, therefore, no danger of drift. It is inactivated rapidly on contact with the soil but kills any green tissues with which it comes into contact.

More toxic and persistent weedkillers should not be used in the home vegetable garden because the risks involved are too great. Whenever using chemicals always follow the manufacturer's instructions.

Mulching

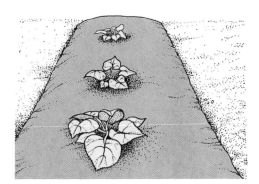

Use black polythene (or organic mulches) to act as a barrier against weed growth, to conserve moisture and to warm up the soil.

Chemical weed control

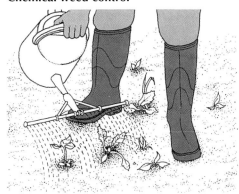

Use a dribble bar for paraquat/diquat at ground level just on top of each weed. Never apply herbicides on a windy day and follow the manufacturer's instructions.

Cloches, tunnels and frames

Cloches are the gardener's allies because they raise the temperature of the soil and air around plants and protect crops against unfavourable weather. This makes it possible to grow a wider range of vegetables successfully and in many cases to harvest them much earlier. Lettuces, for example, can be grown throughout the year and peppers are a possibility in the north of England. At the sowing stage of many crops cloches are extremely helpful. If they are placed over a seedbed a couple of weeks before sowing the soil is warmed up and speedy germination is encouraged. Various crops, such as onions, can be placed under cloches at harvesting time to dry and ripen before storing.

The old type of cloche was bell-shaped and made of very thick glass. Today's protective structures come in a variety of shapes and sizes and they are made of glass, polythene or semi-rigid or clear plastic. Each type has its advantages, but when selecting a cloche certain points should always be considered. It is essential to have ready access to plants under cloches for weeding, training, spraying and harvesting. Except when they are covering small seedlings (see page 15), cloches need not be removed for watering. Water can be applied overhead; it runs down the sides of the cloches, is absorbed into the soil and reaches the roots of the plants, which grow naturally towards sources of food and water.

Heat and light A cloche must retain heat and transmit light. But the retention of heat should not preclude adequate ventilation, and cloches should never be completely airtight. Stagnant air building up underneath them encourages disease. If there is no built-in ventilation, small gaps should be left between individual cloches in rows. However, too much draught and consequent heat loss must also be avoided and it should be possible to close securely the ends of individual cloches or of rows of cloches. Some cloches have end-pieces designed for this purpose.

A cloche must conserve heat and glass types are the best at retaining warmth, although plastic is perfectly adequate in this respect. Glass is also the best transmitter of light, but because it becomes dirty easily glass cloches should be easy to dismantle for regular cleaning.

Size and stability Glass cloches are obviously less likely to be upset by wind than polythene or plastic structures but all types of cloche should have fittings to anchor them securely into the ground if they are exposed to strong winds. Plastic cloches, besides being relatively cheap and comparable in performance to glass, have the advantage of being more easily moved around the vegetable garden and they are probably safer when there are children in the vicinity.

Cloches are available in a variety of shapes and sizes to suit the circumstances and the preferred crops of vegetable growers. Many modern types can be adjusted to several widths and they have side extensions to increase height. The glass or plastic covering of some cloches can be replaced by netting as a protective device against birds.

Polythene tunnels

Polythene sheeting stretched over wire hoops and secured with string or wire is a good, cheap alternative to cloches. It transmits light and retains heat well but it needs replacing as it becomes yellow or torn. The tunnels are simple to erect and transport to different parts of the garden. They can be ventilated by leaving the ends open or by rolling up the sides. Store the sheeting out of sunlight when not in use.

Cold frames

Frames provide virtually the same protection as cloches, although heat is retained better and wind has less effect, making them ideal for hardening off plants initially raised in the greenhouse. However, they are less flexible to use although portable types can be obtained. Modern frames usually have steel or aluminium frames and glass all round. The glass roof, known as a "light", can be hinged or designed to slide back. To retain the most heat a solid-sided frame should be used, whereas for more light glass-to-ground frames are the best. Regular ventilation is more important than for cloches because frames are almost airtight, so prop the lights open and remove them altogether in summer. Poor ventilation may encourage the spread of disease. If the weather is very cold the frames may be covered with sacking at night.

TYPES OF CLOCHE

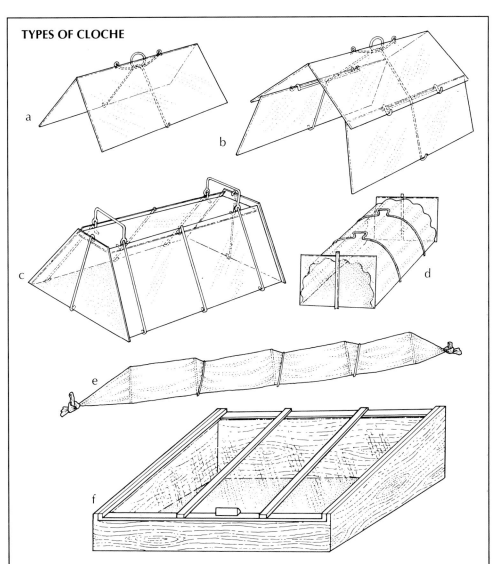

Tent cloche (a) Made of two panes of glass held together with a wire frame.
Barn cloche (b) Shaped as the name suggests, using four panes of glass.
Utility or tomato cloche (c) Flat-topped with three panes of glass.
Corrugated PVC sheeting (d) A strong, long-lasting rigid material which transmits plenty of light and retains heat well.

Polythene film tunnel (e) The cheapest and most satisfactory form of protection. The sheeting is stretched over wire hoops and fixed with strings or wires. It is ventilated by leaving the ends open or by rolling up the sides. A polythene tunnel is easily dismantled and stored.
Cold frame (f) Home-made with a wooden framework and a Dutch "light".

Crop rotation

Growing the same vegetables in the same piece of ground each year eventually results in a build-up of soil-borne pests or diseases. Such continuous growing of brassicas, for example, favours club-root, and successive crops of onions are likely to cause a build-up of stem eelworm.

Different types of vegetables require different ground preparation and cultivation procedures. Potatoes need a deeply cultivated soil which is continually moved during earthing up. On the other hand, root crops – such as carrots, parsnips and beetroot – need a firm, level soil with a fine tilth which is disturbed very little during the growing season.

Fertilizer, lime and manure requirements also vary. Potatoes respond to large applications of organic manure and fertilizer but they should not be limed. Brassica crops also respond to applications of manure and fertilizer but they require a soil between pH 6.5 and 7.5.

These are the major reasons for practising crop rotation in the vegetable garden. It must be said that rotations are easier to effect on paper than they are on the ground.

Grouping the crops

It is useful to put vegetables together in groups which have similar crop protection, cultivation, manure, fertilizer and liming requirements. Groups are then moved

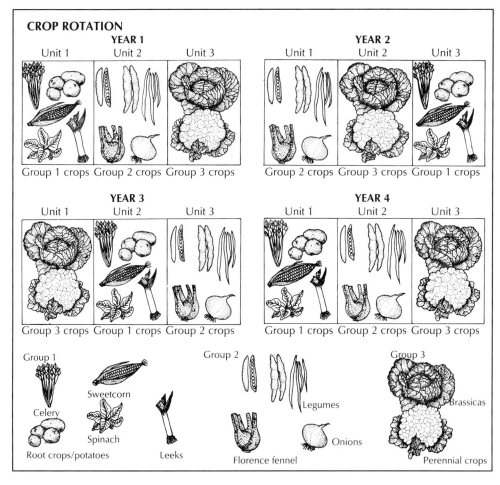

CROP ROTATION

YEAR 1

Unit 1   Unit 2   Unit 3

Group 1 crops   Group 2 crops   Group 3 crops

YEAR 2

Unit 1   Unit 2   Unit 3

Group 2 crops   Group 3 crops   Group 1 crops

YEAR 3

Unit 1   Unit 2   Unit 3

Group 3 crops   Group 1 crops   Group 2 crops

YEAR 4

Unit 1   Unit 2   Unit 3

Group 1 crops   Group 2 crops   Group 3 crops

Group 1

Celery

Sweetcorn

Spinach

Root crops/potatoes

Leeks

Group 2

Legumes

Florence fennel

Onions

Group 3

Brassicas

Perennial crops

sequentially around the vegetable plot so that, over a period of years, a particular piece of ground grows all the crops. In theory it is better to leave as large an interval as possible between growing a crop again on the same site, but it is rarely possible to leave more than three or four years. Thus three and four year rotations have been devised and a three year plan is considered here. A certain amount of compromise is necessary in order to simplify the rotation. Potatoes are grouped with root crops, even though they benefit from applications of organic manure and root crops do not.

Having divided the vegetables in this way, the groups are moved sequentially around the plot over a three year period. The plot is roughly divided into three equal sized units, but an area should be left at one end on which perennial vegetables, such as asparagus and seakale, are grown permanently.

In year one the potato and root crop unit receives no manure or lime but moderately heavy quantities of fertilizer. The legume and onion unit receives heavy dressings of manure and little fertilizer or lime. The brassicas receive average amounts of manure and fertilizer but heavy applications of lime. Crop rotation therefore ensures that all parts of the plot receive manure, fertilizer and lime regularly while the dangers of pest and disease build-up are minimized.

CATCH CROPPING AND INTERCROPPING

Some vegetables grow and mature more quickly than others so there are times of the year when gaps appear in the vegetable plot. These gaps can be used to grow – or catch – a crop of rapidly maturing vegetables. Thus the ground occupied by peas in Unit 2 of the crop rotation plan may not be needed for brassicas until the following spring and can be used for crops such as radishes or endive.

Intercropping Rapidly maturing crops can also be intercropped or grown between slower maturing crops. Spinach can be grown between rows of slow-growing leeks, for example.

Lettuces 1

Lettuce is the salad plant for all seasons. Although an annual that matures naturally during the early summer, the use of suitable varieties, cloches or heated frames, and the correct growing conditions make it possible to harvest lettuce throughout the year.

Types of lettuce
Several different types of lettuce have been bred and they vary considerably in size, form and texture. Three main groups may be recognized although there are intermediates.
Cabbage lettuce These include the butter-heads with globular soft-leaved heads, and the crispheads, also round-headed but with crinkly, crisped leaves. They will usually tolerate poorer and drier soils than the other groups.
Cos lettuce The lettuces of this group are up-right in growth with more or less oblong heads of crips leaves. They grow best in rich, moist soils. Modern varieties do not need to be tied to produce a compact heart.
Leaf lettuce These non-hearting lettuces produce masses of curled foliage but no true heart. The leaves can be picked a few at a time and the plants will continue to grow and produce further leaves for later picking. Some varieties of cos lettuce will continue growing in the same way if closely spaced.

Cultivation
Many modern varieties of lettuce have been specially bred to mature at particular seasons and it is important to select those suitable for the crops required. Depending on the weather and the district, summer- and autumn-maturing lettuce is sown success-ively from late March to early August to mature from June to October. Lettuce sown outdoors in August will mature in November to December if kept under cloches from Sep-tember. Mildew resistant and forcing varieties such as 'Avondefiance' and 'Kwiek' should be used at this time of year. For eating from January to March, lettuce must be sown and raised in a heated (7°C/45°F) greenhouse from November to January, an expensive and often difficult method for most gardeners. Spring lettuce is obtained from winter-hardy varieties and from lettuces grown with cloche or cold frame protection. Sown from August to September to mature in early May, hardy varieties stand throughout the winter without protection although a sheltered position is preferable.

Lettuce sown in October under cloches to mature in April has a more succulent flavour and a higher survival rate, however, as well as the advantage of a slight lead in the harvesting date.
Soil and situation All lettuce varieties prefer an open position in a well-drained and fairly rich soil of pH 6.5-7.5. Lettuces require con-siderable quantities of water during the grow-ing period and the soil must be humus-rich so that it is able to retain and supply moisture for the rapidly growing plants. A soil well manured for a previous crop is ideal, but on poor, thin soils dig in a further dressing of well-rotted compost at a rate of 10-15 lb per square yard when the site is prepared. Apply a balanced general fertilizer at 2 oz per square yard, and before sowing rake the soil to pro-duce a fine tilth.
Sowing To reduce the amount of thinning later, always sow lettuce seed very thinly. Sow in drills ½ in deep at a rate of no more than 10-12 seeds for each 12 in run of drill – hearted lettuces will have a final spacing of 9-12 in apart in the row. Take care not to sow too deeply as this inhibits germination, which should occur within 6-12 days. It is sensible to maintain a regular supply by making frequent sowings with short intervals between, because lettuces, once hearted, do not stand in good condition for very long and soon "bolt" or run to seed.

Spacing
Various spacings and planting patterns are recommended for hearting varieties. The most efficient is to stagger the plants in adjacent rows in a triangular pattern so that the maximum use is made of the land avail-able. Place the plants as 12 in intervals in rows 10 in apart. For dwarf varieties and cloche-grown lettuce spacings of 9 in between the plants and 8 in between the rows may be used. This triangular pattern is particularly valuable for cloche-grown lettuces. If the familiar square pattern with plants opposite one another in adjacent rows is used, the spacings should be 12 in × 12 in, or 9 in × 9 in for dwarf varities. With conventional leaf-

Cabbage types (butterheads)
'All The Year Round',
'Avondefiance' (mildew
resistant), 'Buttercrunch',
'Fortune', 'Suzan', 'Tom Thumb'
(good for small gardens).

**Cabbage types (crispheads/
'Iceberg' types)**
'El Toro', 'Lakeland Wonder',
'Target', 'Webbs Wonderful'.

Cos types
'Little Gem' (good for small
gardens), 'Lobjoit's Green Cos',
'Winter Density'.

VARIETIES OF LETTUCE

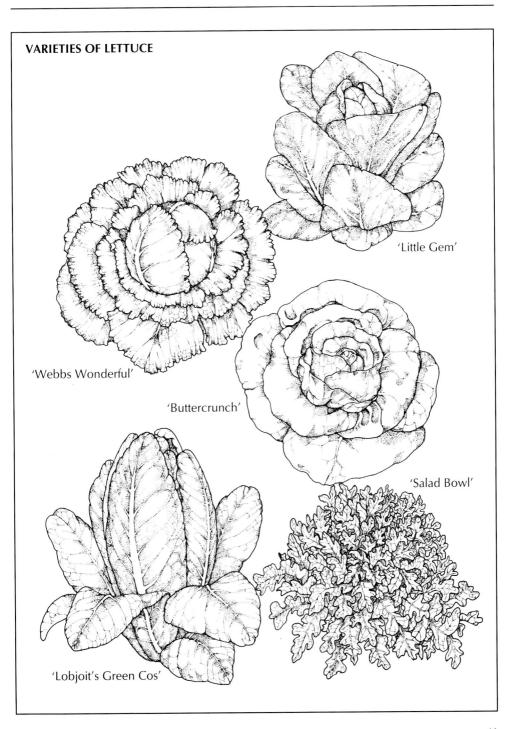

'Little Gem'

'Webbs Wonderful'

'Buttercrunch'

'Salad Bowl'

'Lobjoit's Green Cos'

Lettuces 2

lettuce of the 'Salad Bowl' type, spacings are similar to those given for hearting varieties. Some cos lettuces, however, will produce good leaf lettuce during spring and summer with only 5-6 in between the rows and 1 in between individual plants.

Thinning and transplanting Direct-sown crops should be thinned as soon as the seedlings are large enough to handle. Never let the seedlings become overcrowded as this will check growth. There is a tendency to grow more lettuce than can be consumed and this is particularly true with sown crops. Trans-

planting allows more control. The method of plant raising is critical, however, since any check to growth at transplanting may easily lead to "bolting". "Bolting" – premature running to flower – is induced by high temperatures (over 21°C/70°F) and dry conditions. Lettuce transplants for outside should always be raised in small individual peat pots or blocks and never grown in a seedbed for bare-root planting. Sow lettuce seed in a 3½ in pot every ten days and prick out as many seedlings as necessary into pots or blocks. Do this at the first true leaf stage.

LEAF LETTUCE

'Salad Bowl' is the conventional leaf lettuce but certain cos varieties ('Lobjoit's Green', 'Paris White' and 'Valmaine') can also be grown successfully for leafing. Closely spaced, they can produce good leaf in 40-50 days compared with the 60-80 days required for other lettuce.

They also have the advantage of growing again from the base to provide a second crop. Grown this way, one square yard of leaf lettuce sown each week from April to mid-May, and again from mid-July to the end of August, will produce lettuce leaves throughout summer and early autumn.

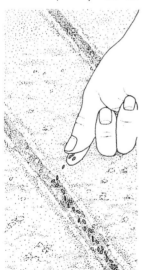 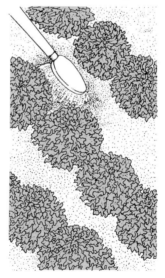 

1 April to mid-May. At weekly intervals sow the seed in ½ in drills, 4-5 in apart in the prepared seedbed, allowing 10-15 plants per 12 in of drill.

2 Early May to June. Allow the seedlings to develop unchecked without thinning. Water in dry weather. Spray aphids and diseases as required.

3 Late May to late June. Harvest the leaves by cutting them off near ground level. Leave stumps to re-grow.

LEAF LETTUCE
'Cerise' (red, oak leaf type),
'Frisby' (green), 'Lollo Rossa' (red
frilled type), 'Salad Bowl' (green,
oak leaf type).

PROTECTED LETTUCE
'Kellys' (crisphead/'Iceberg' type),
'Kwiek' (butterhead), 'Marbello'
(crisphead/'Iceberg' type),
'Novita' (curly leaf type).

Keep the seedlings cool to produce short, sturdy plants and transplant them when they have four or five true leaves.

Watering The best crops are produced when there has been no check to growth. The quality and size of the crop will be improved greatly by weekly applications of 3-4 gal of water per square yard in dry weather. If this is not possible a single application at the same rate 7-10 days before they are due to mature will increase the size of the lettuce heads markedly in spring and summer. Over-wintered lettuce should not normally need additional watering.

Try to water in the morning, and on sunny, drying days if possible, so that the leaves are dry by nightfall. Lettuces that are wet overnight are more vulnerable to disease.

Pests and diseases
Birds, slugs and cutworms may be troublesome but can be controlled by the methods described on pages 31-33. Leaf aphids may be controlled by the use of systemic aphicides such as pirimicarb or heptenophos or derris or pyrethrum if the plants are near maturity. Some varieties such as 'Avoncrisp' and 'Avondefiance' are resistant to lettuce root aphids. Mancozeb spray may be used against downy mildew. Remove infected plants carefully so that fungal spores are not spread onto healthy lettuce plants.

Botrytis cinerea or grey mould may be a problem on lettuce in damp, cool weather. Affected plants should be removed and destroyed, which is more likely to occur if plants are grown close together, preventing good air circulation.

Lettuce viruses show up either as a mosaic or pronounced vein network on the leaves. Destroy infected plants because there is no really effective method of control. Remove weeds, which may harbour viruses, and control any aphids which appear.

Protected lettuce

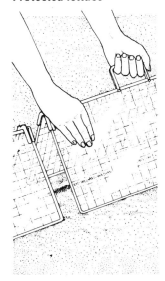  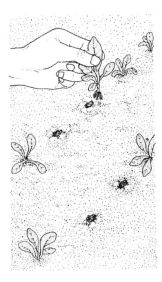

1 Mid-October. Sow 3-4 seeds ½ in deep at 3 in intervals in drills 8 in apart in the prepared seedbed, and place cloches over the drills.

2 Late October. When the seedlings are ½ in high, thin each group, leaving the strongest plant at each position. Ventilate well during the winter.

3 Late February. As growth begins again thin to 9 in (6 in for dwarf varieties). In dry weather, water the plants 7-10 days before harvesting, March to April.

Lettuces 3

Spring lettuce

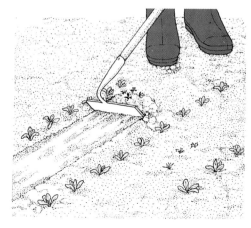

1 Late August to early September. Sow the seed thinly in ½ in drills 10 in apart in the prepared seedbed. Cover the drills.

2 Mid to late September. When the seedlings are ½ in high thin to 2-3 in apart. Hoe between the rows once or twice in winter.

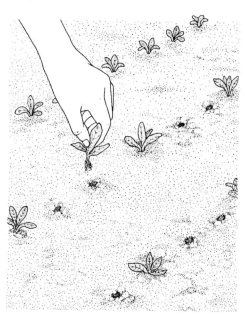

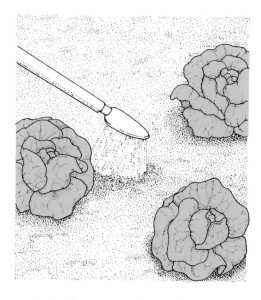

3 Late February to early March. Thin the plants to the full distance for each variety so that they alternate in adjacent rows if possible. Apply a top dressing of balanced fertilizer at 2 oz per square yard.

4 Late April. In dry weather apply 3-4 gal of water per square yard 7-10 days before likely maturity, which should be from early May onwards.

Summer lettuce

1 Late March to early August. In the prepared seedbed take out ½ in drills 10 in apart (8 in for dwarf varieties) and sow the seed thinly. Cover the drill.

2 April to mid-August. When the seedlings are ½-1 in high, thin to 12 in (9 in for dwarf varieties). Alternate the seedlings in adjacent rows.

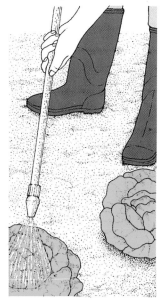

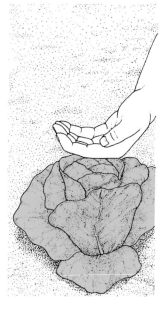

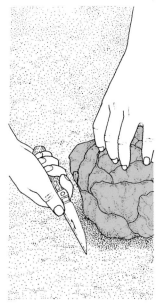

3 May to September/ October. In dry weather apply 3-4 gal of water per square yard each week. Spray against aphids as required.

4 June to October. Push hearting lettuces gently with the back of the hand to test for firmness. Squeezing between the fingers damages the hearts.

5 June to October. When firm, harvest by cutting the plants below the lower leaves. Alternatively, pull up whole plants and trim off roots.

Endive/Celtuce

Endive is a hardy annual plant of the same genus as chicory. It is grown for the use of its leaves in salads and it requires blanching to be palatable. Endive can be grown over a long season and it is most valuable as an autumn and winter vegetable.

Cultivation
Endive needs a good medium to light soil that has been deeply winter dug and, preferably, manured for a previous crop. Choose an open position except for spring-sown crops, which may bolt unless grown in partial shade.

Sowing For successive blanchings sow batches of seed every three to four weeks from March until August. Sow the seed in ½ in deep drills that are 12 in apart. As soon as the first true leaves appear, thin the seedlings, leaving the curly-leaved varieties 9 in apart and the broad-leaved varieties 12 in apart. Water the growing plants regularly, as for lettuce, especially during dry hot weather, because drought encourages endive to run to seed. When the plants are fully grown,

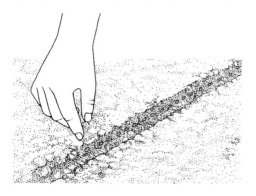

1 Late March to August. Sow the seed very thinly in ½ in drills 12 in apart.

2 When the first true leaves appear, thin the seedlings until they are 9-12 in apart.

CELTUCE

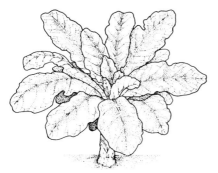

Celtuce is a mutant or sport of lettuce which grows on a short stem. As its name suggests it combines two vegetables in one. The stems are used in the same way as celery and the leaves can be substituted for lettuce.

Celtuce requires a humus-rich soil of pH 6.5-7.5 and, to ensure this, compost or manure should be incorporated during winter digging. Sow the seed from late March until June or July at two week intervals in shallow ½ in drills that are 12 in apart. When the seedlings are about 1 in high thin them until they are 9 in apart. Celtuce needs to be well watered because otherwise the leaves become tough. In hot dry weather celtuce resists bolting better than most ordinary lettuce.

Pick celtuce leaves as soon as they form on the plants, but never pick the plants completely bare because this severely weakens them. The stems are ready from June onwards or within three months of the sowing date. Cut the stalks when they are about 1 in thick at the plant's base.

ENDIVE
SUMMER
'Minerva'.
AUTUMN/WINTER
'Ione', 'Moss Curled', 'Sally'

CELTUCE
No named varieties available.

about 12 weeks after sowing (July to October), make sure they are dry and tie them loosely with raffia to keep the lower leaves off the ground and lessen the risk of rotting. Then begin to blanch two or three plants at a time to provide a convenient supply over a longer period. Place a large plastic pot over each plant to exclude light completely. Remember to cover the pots' drainage holes with a tile or stones and leave a slight gap between the rims and the soil for ventilation. The blanched leaves should be sweet and edible within 2-3 weeks, although they take twice as long in winter.

Winter endive Hardy broad-leaved varieties of endive can be sown in frames or under cloches in late August or early September for winter use until March or April.

Harvesting

Cut the plants with a sharp knife just above soil level when the leaves are a creamy-white colour. Use blanched endive immediately because it does not keep well.

3 July to October. Loosely tie the fully grown plants with raffia.

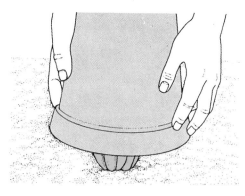

4 At the same time, select some plants for blanching. Place plastic pots over them.

5 Cover the pots' drainage holes to exclude all light. Leave a slight gap between each pot's rim and the soil for ventilation.

6 After 2-3 weeks when the leaves are creamy-white cut the plants off just above soil level with a sharp knife.

Chicory

Chicory is a hardy perennial plant related to the dandelion. Forcing varieties are sown in early May, lifted in October and then grown in complete darkness to produce the blanched chicons (tightly bunched groups of leaves) which may be used for salads throughout the winter. Ground, dried chicory roots are also used as a substitute or additive for coffee, especially in France. Blanching is usually required to make the leaves palatable although there are some varieties of chicory, such as 'Sugar Loaf', which produce sweet flavoured leaves without blanching. Chicory is seldom troubled by pests and diseases.

Cultivation

Chicory grows best in a medium to light soil that is moderately rich. Soil manured for a previous crop is ideal. Do not incorporate any manure or compost into the ground just before sowing, however, because this encourages forked roots which are less suitable for forcing. The seedbed should be in an open position. A few days before sowing apply a general, balanced fertilizer at 1oz per square yard, then rake the soil to a fine tilth.

Sowing In May or June sow the seed of forcing varieties thinly in ½ in drills that are 9-12 in apart. When the first true leaves appear thin the seedlings until they are 8 in apart in the row and hoe regularly to keep down weeds.

Storing From October to November when the foliage has died down lift the parsnip-like roots for storing prior to forcing. Discard any

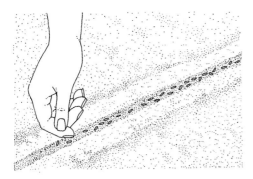

1 Early May. Sow the seed thinly in ½ in drills that are 9-12 in apart.

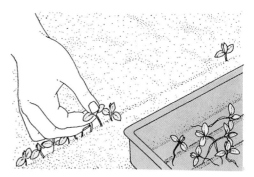

2 When the first true leaves appear thin the seedlings until they are 8 in apart.

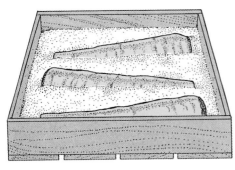

5 Store the prepared roots horizontally in boxes of dry sand in a cool frost-free shed.

6 Mid-November. At weekly intervals plant three or four roots in a 9 in dia. pot of sand, keeping ½ in of each crown above the soil.

thin or forked roots and retain those that are 1-1½in in diameter at the top because these are most suitable for forcing. Cut off any remaining leaves to within ½ in of the crown and trim the root ends and side roots, leaving a length of 9 in. Pack the roots in boxes of dry sand in a cool frost-free place.

Blanching

Stored chicory roots need to be forced in complete darkness to produce creamy-white chicons. From mid-November onwards remove a few roots for blanching at weekly intervals to provide a continual supply throughout winter until the end of March. Plant them in plastic pots (9 in dia.) filled with sand or light garden soil, making sure that ½ in of crown is above the surface. Water them sparingly and then completely cover them with black polythene to exclude all light. Light causes greening of the young leaves and results in a bitter taste. Keep the sand or soil moist but never wet it, and put the pots in a well-ventilated cellar or shed with a tempature of 7°-13°C/45°-55°F.

Harvesting

The blanched chicons should be ready for cutting within four weeks. Cut or snap them off just above soil level and use them immediately. After the chicons have been harvested, the roots will produce several smaller shoots that are very acceptable for salads if blanched in the same way.

3 October to November. When the leaves are dying lift the roots with a fork.

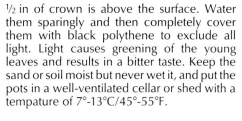

4 Cut off remaining leaves to ½ in of the crown and discard unsuitable roots. Shorten the roots to 9 in and remove any side roots.

7 Water the roots sparingly and cover the top of the pot with black polythene to exclude all light. Place in a well ventilated shed at a temperature of 7°-13°C/45°-55°F.

8 Mid-December to mid-February. Cut or snap off the chicons just above the soil surface about four weeks after planting.

Growing brassicas

Admirably suited to the climate of northern Europe, the brassicas, such as cabbages, Brussels sprouts, cauliflowers, broccoli and kale, are key plants in any vegetable grower's plot. Certain general principles apply to their cultivation. Most brassicas, except some varieties of kale and chinese cabbage, should be raised in a special brassica seedbed and then transplanted, usually 5-7 weeks later, to a permanent bed. This saves space, because the main brassica plots can be used for other vegetables while the seedlings are growing. Alternatively, buy young brassica plants ready for planting out.

Brassicas need a fertile soil and they should not be grown in the same plot more than one year in three. Move them around each year, preferably to ground where peas or beans have been grown the previous year (see page 38). Peas and beans leave nitrogen in the soil at a level which suits brassicas. The other reason for keeping brassicas on the move in the danger of previous infections of club-root lingering on in the soil. Another, resistant, vegetable can be grown in a plot which has suffered from club-root. Brassica crops must not be grown again in an affected plot for at least seven years.

Dig the ground early in winter and leave it to consolidate. All brassicas need firm ground. If the area has been dug shortly before sowing or planting, work it over with a three-pronged hand cultivator and firm it down well with the feed. All brassicas need a pH of 6.5-7.5.

The seedbed
The seedbed should be in an open, sunny but sheltered position. Ideally, make a seedbed on soil manured for a previous crop. If this is not possible, in autumn apply well-rotted manure or garden compost (1 bucketful per square yard) and leave the plot to weather over the winter. Before sowing rake in a balanced general fertilizer at a rate of 2 oz per square yard. At the same time apply chlorpyrifos, pirimiphos-methyl or lindane to combat cabbage root fly. Firm the soil and rake to produce a fine tilth.

Sowing If the seedbed is dry, water thoroughly before sowing. Use a foot-board to avoid compacting the surface of the bed while sowing. Mark out shallow drills 6 in apart and draw out the drills ¾-1 in deep. Dust the seed with captan before sowing to control damping-off disease. Mark each row with sticks, placing a label with sowing date and variety,

1 Lift the seedlings carefully, taking care not to damage the roots. Dip the roots in calomel paste.

2 Plant the seedlings at the spacing given for each brassica and check they are firmly planted by gently tugging an upper leaf.

written in indelible ink. Germination takes 7-12 days. Keep the seedlings free from weeds, and water them during dry weather. Thin the seedlings to 1-2 in apart as soon as they can be handled. Firm back the soil after thinning.

The permanent (planting) bed

Double-dig the permanent brassica plot in winter and dress it with 10-15 lb per square yard of well-rotted manure or compost. Experiments have shown that a marked increase in yield can result from preparing soils deeply for brassicas. The roots of Brussels sprouts, for instance, penetrate 36 in or more into deeply dug soils. Although it is seldom practical to dig the plot to this depth, double-dig it if possible to a depth of 18-24 in. Brassicas are greedy for water, and deep digging allows their root systems to develop and extract more water from lower levels in the soil. It also reduces the uptake of water from the upper soil layers, which remain moist for longer than would be the case with shallower digging.

Transplanting

The young brassicas are ready to transplant 5-7 weeks after sowing, when they have 3-4 leaves and are 4-6 in tall. The day before transplanting, water the seedlings thoroughly so that they lift easily with minimum damage to the roots.

Lift the seedlings carefully so that the roots are disturbed as little as possible. Cover them with sacking or polythene so that they do not dry out before being planted. Dip the roots of the seedlings in thiophanate-methyl to control club-root. Plant the seedlings with a trowel or hand fork at the appropriate distance for the brassica concerned. The prepared plot should be watered thoroughly the day before planting takes place. Firm the soil around the roots by hand. Water the plants in, using a rose on the can or, if the weather is dry, prepare planting holes and "puddle" in the young plants. Make sure they are firm by tugging the upper leaf gently. Water them, if necessary, until they become established, placing 1/4 pint of water around the base of each plant daily. In hot, sunny weather protect the transplants by covering them with newspaper or hessian during the day to cut down the transpiration rate. Within three days of planting-out apply pirimiphos-methyl, lindane or chlorpyrifos to the soil around the plants as a further insurance against cabbage root fly.

3 In dry weather prepare planting holes and puddle in the young plants.

4 Apply a suitable insecticide to the soil at each plant's base within 3 days of planting. Water until they are established.

Cabbages 1

Cabbage is a biennial plant and the most widely grown brassica. Individual tastes can be satisfied throughout the year with the five types available. Spring cabbage is hardy and is appreciated as an early green vegetable. Summer cabbage provides a welcome alternative to summer salads. Winter cabbage, including savoys, is easy to grow and is hardy. Apart from its pickling qualities, red cabbage is delicious as a cooked autumn vegetable. The increasingly-popular, autumn-harvested Chinese cabbage can be cooked (with little aroma) or used in salads.

Spring cabbage

Spring cabbage is sown or planted in late summer to mature in spring. "Spring greens" are simply closely-planted spring cabbages eaten before they heart up.

Sowing The seed is sown in late July (northern Britain or cold areas) or early August (southern or milder districts) as explained on page 50. The seedlings are transplanted to their final quarters from mid-September or mid-October in rows 12 in apart and with 12 in between the plants in each row if hearted cabbages are required.

Spring greens If space is limited and spring greens are required plant them at 4 in intervals in the rows. The plants can either be left to produce unhearted greens, or two out of every three plants can be removed and used for greens in early spring while the remaining plants, now spaced at 12 in by 12 in, will heart up for use later. Wider row spacings are often recommended but these give a lesser yield.

Firm planting is important and a few weeks after planting it is useful to pull a little soil around the stems to give some additional protection against frost-lifting in the winter. No fertilizer should be given at this stage and, apart from keeping the plot free from weeds, the only attention they need until growth starts the following spring is to firm back plants loosened by frost or other adverse weather.

In early March, if the weather is good, apply and water in a dressing of nitrate of soda or sulphate of ammonia at a rate of 2 oz per square yard. This encourages rapid growth as the weather becomes warmer. Alternatively, in nitrogen-rich soils, a balanced fertilizer can be used at the same rate.

Harvesting

The crop may be harvested as required. In mild seasons spring greens are ready in February while in late seasons hearted cabbages stand until early June. In some cold areas cloches may be used to protect spring cabbages over winter.

Summer cabbage

Summer cabbage is sown between February and May for harvesting from late July until autumn. When deciding how much to grow, remember that it matures at the same time as many other vegetables, including peas and beans.The seedbed and the permanent plot should be well prepared in late February. Sowing in frames during February for planting out in April provides the earliest crops, but seeds are normally sown in the open from March to May.

Sowing Sow the seed thinly in $3/4$-1 in deep drills 6 in apart. Water the drills beforehand to encourage speedy germination and if the weather is warm and dry, dust the drills with derris, pirimiphos-methyl or lindane as the seedlings emerge as a precaution against flea beetle. Summer cabbages are very vulnerable to cabbage root fly and it is important to apply appropriate control measures against this and club-root at both the sowing and transplanting stages (see page 50).

Transplanting From April to May dip the seedlings in thiophanate-methyl and plant in the permanent bed, at 18 in intervals in rows 18 in apart for large-headed varieties or at 14 in intervals in rows 14 in apart for smaller-headed varieties. Firm the seedlings into their holes and water thoroughly.

When the plants have settled down, and are well-established, apply and water in a balanced fertilizer, such as a brand of Growmore, at 2 oz per square yard. Throughout the growing season, hoe between the rows with a Dutch hoe to keep down weeds and maintain a water-conserving tilth. If necessary spray or dust to control any pests or diseases that occur, such as caterpillars and aphids.

Harvesting

Hearted summer cabbages are ready for cutting from late July until autumn. Cut with a sharp knife just above soil level.

TYPES OF CABBAGE

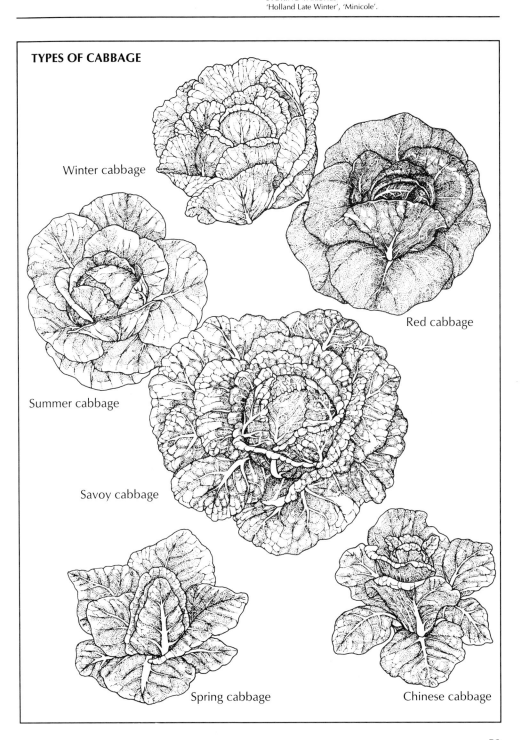

Winter cabbage

Red cabbage

Summer cabbage

Savoy cabbage

Spring cabbage

Chinese cabbage

Cabbages 2

Spring cabbage

1 July to August. Take out ¾-1 in deep drills, 6 in apart in a prepared seedbed. Sprinkle a suitable insecticide along the drills and water them thoroughly.

2 July to August. Sow the seed thinly and cover with a fine tilth.

3 Mid-September to mid-October. Prepare holes at 12 in intervals (4 in for spring greens) in the permanent bed.

6 Throughout the growing season hoe between the rows regularly to keep them weed-free and maintain a good tilth.

7 Earl March. Spread and then hoe in 2 oz of nitrate of soda or sulphate of ammonia to encourage hearting.

4 Then plant the seedlings (previously dipped in thiophanate-methyl) and water in well. Rows should be 12 in apart in rows.

5 About 2 weeks after planting pull up a little soil around the base of each plant to protect against frost-lifting. Firm any plants loosened later by adverse weather.

Spring greens

8 April to June. Cut spring cabbages as required. Clear away any stumps and roots.

Mid-March. To obtain spring greens, remove 2 plants out of 3. Those remaining will heart up for later use.

Cabbages 3

Winter cabbage

Winter cabbages are sown in April or May and harvested from late autumn to the following March or April. They include the savoys, which are easily recognized by their dark green, wrinkled leaves. All the varieties are easy to grow and hardy, succeeding better on poor soils than most other brassicas. Apart from the times of sowing, transplanting and maturing their cultivation differs little from that of summer cabbage.

Sowing In May sow the seed very thinly in 3/4-1 in drills that are 6 in apart. Water the drills before sowing.

Transplanting In July transplant the seedlings to the permanent bed, which should have been enriched with fertilizer a few weeks before (see page 50). Plant the seedlings at 18 in intervals in rows 18 in apart. If the weather is very dry, pour a little water into each hole before putting the plants down. Remember also to protect against cabbage root fly (see page 31) when setting out the seedlings and firming them in well.

Water the growing plants frequently during the summer and hoe lightly between the rows to keep down the weeds.

Harvesting

From October until early spring, cut the individual heads as they mature.

Red cabbage

Red cabbage is sown in the spring at the same time as summer cabbage but it needs a slightly longer growing season and it is not harvested until the autumn. It can also be treated like spring cabbage – sown in August and transplanted in March to mature in the summer. Before sowing, work out what is needed because a few plants are enough for pickling purposes. Cultivate red cabbage in the same way as summer cabbage. Sow the seed very thinly in March or April and transplant in April or May, 12-15 in each way.

Harvesting

Red cabbage is ready from September onwards. Be sure to cut the mature heads well before there is any danger of severe frost.

Red cabbage can be stored for several months in a cool, frost-free place.

HARVESTING AND STORING CABBAGE

Some types of cabbage, especially the almost white, tight-headed Dutch varities, can be stored after harvesting in November or December. They will keep until April but should be inspected for blemishes or rot two or three times during the winter.

1 Lift the whole plant up with a fork when the heart is firm to the touch.

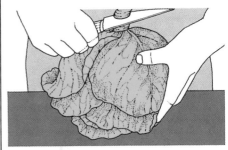

2 Cut off the roots and stem and remove the coarse outer leaves.

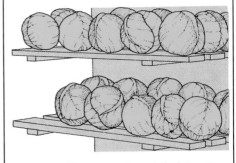

3 Store cabbages on slatted shelving, in heaps if required, in a frost-free shed.

Chinese cabbage

Chinese cabbage is a versatile vegetable that is easier to grow than other vegetables in the brassica group and has a relatively short growing season. The general principles of brassica growing (page 50) apply. It is especially important to have a moisture-retentive, rich seedbed because Chinese cabbage is not transplanted and matures in the area where it has been sown.

Sowing in July, sow 2-3 of the large seeds at 8-9 in intervals in ¾-1 in deep drills, 12 in apart. When the seedlings emerge thin to one plant per station.

Keep them well watered because they may "bolt" in hot summer weather. Do not water, however, if the weather is wet, as this may cause "splitting" of the heads. When the plants begin to heart up in August, tie the leaves together with raffia. This is not necessary with self-hearting varieties.

Harvesting

From September to November cut the heads just above soil level with a knife.

1 Early July. Dribble water into the ¾-1 in deep drills, 12 in apart, and sow 2-3 seeds at 9 in intervals.

2 July. Thin each group of seedlings to leave a single plant at each station. Apply an insecticide around the base of each plant.

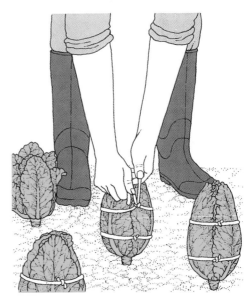

3 August. When the plants begin to heart up tie the outer leaves together with raffia. Keep them well watered.

Brussels sprouts 1

Brussels sprouts are popular and hardy brassicas, and in Britain they are a traditional ingredient in the Christmas dinner. In recent years F_1 hybrids have been bred, mostly of compact growth, that mature all their uniform "button" sprouts at the same time. While these are ideal for the freezer, most gardeners still grow some of the open pollinated, conventional varieties. With these, the sprouts mature a few at a time on individual plants, so picking may be carried out over a period of several months. This is important for growers without freezers, who may require only a pound or two at a time.

A good selection of varieties will provide harvests of sprouts from September to early March or even April, but the most useful crops are gathered from October to February because few other fresh vegetables are available at this time.

Cultivation

The general principles of brassica growing apply to Brussels sprouts (see page 50). An open position, in full sun but sheltered from strong winds, is most suitable although they will tolerate slight shade. A firm soil is important because Brussels sprouts may grow to 3 ft or more and good root anchorage is essential for them to stand through the winter. In light soils earthing up the stems slightly about a month after transplanting helps to anchor them, but in exposed areas staking is sometimes necessary.

Soil and situation Brussels sprouts grow best on fertile soil that has been deeply dug and well manured the previous winter. As they are not usually planted out until May, another crop is often taken from the same land beforehand. This site should be dug over about a week before planting and a dressing of 2 oz per square yard of a balanced general fertilizer raked in. The seed is sown in the brassica seedbed during March or early April and the seedlings are transplanted in May or early June to the prepared site. March-sown seedlings may need cloche protection if the weather is still very harsh.

Sowing Sow the seed thinly in 3/4-1 in drills that are spaced 6 in apart. The seed is sown thinly to prevent overcrowding and to encourage strong plants, which are necessary

for the successful growth of this tall, top-heavy vegetable. Brussels sprouts are vulnerable to club-root and cabbage root fly and the same control measures given for cabbages must be applied at both the sowing and transplanting stages. Seeds sown under cloches or frames in February for planting out in April will give an earlier crop. This method is useful for producing sprouts in September in addition to the main crop sown in the open to provide autumn and winter sprouts.

F_1 hybrids If F_1 hybrids to produce button sprouts for freezing are being grown, spacings of 20 in between the rows and 20 in between plants can be used. This provides a good yield from a relatively small area for picking at one time. Remove the growing point and smaller leaves when the lower sprouts are about 1/2 in across to encourage most of them to mature at the same time. For the "cut and come again" requirement of most gardeners, spacings of 36 in × 36 in are used. Grown at these distances most varieties produce an excellent crop while allowing easy access for picking. There appears

3 At the same time, puddle in the young plants and check that they are firmly planted by gently tugging each top leaf.

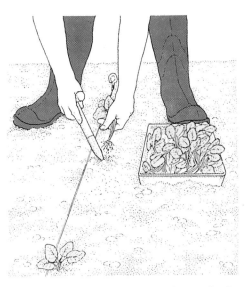

1 Late May to early June. Dig over the planting site and rake in a balanced, general fertilizer, such as a proprietary brand of Growmore, at 2 oz per square yard.

2 Transplant the seedlings from the seedbed into rows 36 in apart with 36 in (20 in × 20 in for F₁ hybrids) between plants. Plant them firmly with the lowest leaf at soil level.

4 June. Apply a suitable insecticide to the soil at the base of the plants to combat cabbage root fly.

5 June. Continue to water the young plants until they are well established.

Brussels sprouts 2

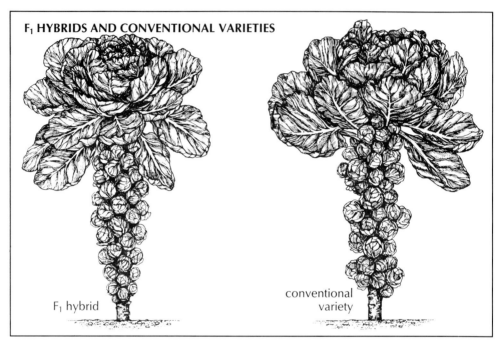

F₁ HYBRIDS AND CONVENTIONAL VARIETIES

F₁ hybrid

conventional variety

6 July. In light soils or exposed sites draw up a little soil round the base of each stem. Hoe regularly to keep the plants free from weeds.

7 July. Apply a foliar feed or water in a high potash fertilizer at a rate of 1 oz per square yard. Spray with dimethoate, pirimicarb or heptenophos to control aphid attacks.

to be no advantage in closer spacing unless dwarf varieties are used, when spacings of 2½ ft each way are sufficient. Firm planting is essential and the seedlings should be set with the lowest leaves at soil level to help establish a good root system. Water or puddle in the young plants. Check that they are firmly established by tugging gently at the top leaf of each plant.

Although additional watering during the growing season is often beneficial to cabbages, there appears to be no advantage in watering Brussels sprouts regularly unless the weather is very dry. Brussels sprout plants are in the ground for a long period, so regular weeding and hoeing should be carried out and any necessary pest and disease controls should be applied as necessary.

Aphids and cabbage whitefly are often particularly troublesome and if left can spoil the developing sprouts. Aphids must be sprayed as soon as they are spotted, or they will penetrate the sprouts themselves. Wood pigeons may attack the sprouts. A system of stakes carrying netting will protect the growing crop against birds and help to support the plants. Application of a foliar feed or a high potash fertilizer in July is often beneficial, particularly on light soils.

Harvesting
As the sprouts mature, remove any yellowing leaves from the lower part of the stem to improve air circulation. Pick or cut the sprouts when they are still tight and about the size of a walnut. Start picking from the base. When all the sprouts have been picked from a stem, use the Brussels sprout tops as "winter greens".

Aftercare
Surplus leaves can go on the compost heap, but the woody stems should be pulled up with the roots, dried and burned at the end of the season.

Do not leave Brussels sprouts in the ground to flower and seed, because they will continue to draw up nutrients from the soil and leave an unnecessarily large deficit for the crop that follows them.

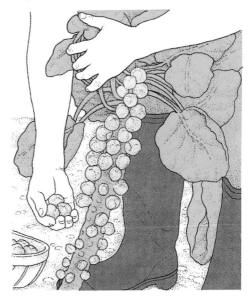

8 September onwards. Remove yellowing leaves from the stems, and any "blown" (loose and open) sprouts.

9 As soon as the buttons are firm, gather them as required from the bottom of the stem.

Cauliflowers 1

Gardeners are often confused about the differences between cauliflowers, sprouting broccoli and calabrese and the various times they are in season.

Cauliflowers are distinguished, for practical purposes, by their large heads of tightly packed white, immature flowers known as "curds". Different varieties mature successively virtually throughout the year and they can be divided into three basic groups: summer, autumn and winter cauliflowers. The latter is also known as broccoli or heading broccoli. It is easy to understand how confusion has arisen, but sprouting broccoli is distinct from heading broccoli in that it produces groups of smaller, leafy flowerheads on short stalks and it is these young "spears" of succulent leaves and immature flowers that are eaten.

Broccoli is Italian for "little stalks", so it is better to restrict this term to the purple and white sprouting broccolis that are in season from January to May. Calabrese is structurally intermediate, producing a fairly large central green curd and a number of smaller sprouts that grow once the central head is cut.

Cauliflowers

A favourite among brassicas, the cauliflower is one of the more difficult vegetables to grow successfully because it is demanding in its soil, moisture and food requirements.

Soil and situation A deeply dug, fertile soil rich in humus is essential to obtain crops of good quality. The general principles of brassica growing apply – thorough soil preparation with heavy dressings of manure helping to provide food and retain moisture during the growing period (see page 50). The pH of the soil should be between 6.5 and 7.5 and the site should be open but not exposed. Cauliflowers are less hardy than other brassicas and in severe weather even the over-wintered varieties may be severely damaged or killed. They require ample food during their period of growth and, in addition to the manure dug in during the winter, a dressing of 2-3 oz per square yard of a general fertilizer should be raked into the soil before planting.

Cauliflower ssedlings need careful handling and firm planting. They should never be short of water or they will produce small, premature heads of poor quality. Applications of

Summer cauliflower

1 Winter. Dig the soil deeply, incorporating a dressing of 15-20 lb per square yard of well-rotted manure.

2 Late March to early April (frame-raised plants) or early to mid-June (plants raised from seed sown outdoors in March to April). Rake in a dressing of 2-3 oz per square yard of a balanced fertilizer 1-2 weeks before planting.

SUMMER
'All The Year Round', 'Alpha', 'Mayflower'.

SUMMER/AUTUMN
'Barrier Reef', 'Plana', 'Violet Queen' (purple heads), 'Wallaby'.

WINTER (HEADING BROCCOLI)
'Arcade', 'Purple Cape' (purple heads), 'Walcheren Winter 3'.

up to 4 gal of water per square yard during dry periods improve the quality and yield. To maintain healthy, vigorous growth a dressing of 1 oz per square yard of sulphate of ammonia should be watered in when the young plants are well established but before the curds start to form. As with other brassicas, club-root, cabbage root fly and downy mildew (see page 29) may be troublesome and the appropriate control measures should be applied as a matter of routine.

Summer cauliflowers mature from June to August and may be raised in several ways depending on the facilities available. The easiest is to sow the seed in the open in March or early April for transplanting in June to crop in August or even September.

Early cauliflowers
Crops in June and July may be obtained by sowing seed in January in gentle heat (13°C/55°F). As soon as the seedlings are large enough to handle they are pricked out into cold frames 3 in by 3 in apart or into 3-3½ in pots of John Innes compost No. 1 (or equivalent) which are then kept in frames or a cold glasshouse. After a few days the frame is ventilated so that sturdy, healthy plants are produced. These are hardened off for planting in their final quarters in March. Alternatively, if no heat is available, seed can be sown the previous September and the seedlings pricked out into frames to over-winter before being hardened off for March planting.

Maximum yield of summer cauliflower is dependent on water supply. If the crop can be watered frequently, the spacing can be as close as 18 in by 18 in. In drier conditions, spacings of 24 in by 24 in are better.

Autumn cauliflowers
Autumn cauliflowers are in season from September to December and are sown outdoors in seedbeds during April and May for transplanting in late June to their final quarters. Their cultivation is similar to that of summer cauliflowers, differing only in their spacing requirements. The large, vigorous varieties are best planted at spacings of 27 in by 27 in but the newer, smaller Australian varieties can be spaced more closely, at 21 in by 21 in.

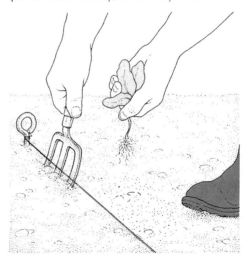

3 Water the seedlings in the seedbed or frame the day before lifting them for transplanting. Lift them carefully and dip roots in calomel, carbendazim or thiophanate-methyl.

4 Plant the seedlings at 24 in intervals in rows 24 in apart on the prepared site, watered on the previous day. Water or puddle in the transplanted seedlings. Check that they are firmly planted by tugging the uppermost leaf of each.

Cauliflowers 2

Winter cauliflowers

Winter cauliflowers are not quite so demanding in their soil and moisture requirements as summer and autumn cauliflowers, which do not thrive on dry soils or when moisture is lacking. On heavy soils the problem is often an excess of water because they do not tolerate "wet feet". They are also unlikely to survive periods of prolonged frost, and the early winter varieties, such as those in the Roscoff group, are not fully hardy in Britain and may be killed in severe weather. Depending on the varieties used, winter cauliflowers mature between December and late May or early June. Most gardeners choose to grow varieties that mature from March onwards unless they are in favoured parts of Britain, where home-grown cauliflowers can be enjoyed at Christmas and in the New Year. In cold areas where winter cauliflowers do not thrive, hardy sprouting broccoli should be grown to fill the winter and early spring gap. Cultivation requirements for winter cauliflowers are very similar to those of the summer and autumn varieties, although it is a much slower-maturing crop.

Sowing The seed is thinly sown in prepared seedbeds from mid-April to mid-May and transplanted during June and July into firm ground, well-manured for a previous crop and dressed with 2-3 oz per square yard of a general balanced fertilizer about a week before planting.

Planting distances for winter cauliflowers should be 30 in between the rows with 30 in between the plants. The usual control measures to combat club-root and cabbage root fly should be applied.

Winter cauliflower has a long growing season and needs plenty of nourishment. If growth is slow, further feeding may be necessary. Water in a mixture of 2 oz of superphosphate and 1 oz of sulphate of potash per square yard to improve growth during late summer. The plants must be grown hard to withstand the winter so nitrogen fertilizers that encourage soft growth late in the season should not be given.

As the curds form and begin to swell it is helpful to protect them against hard weather by snapping one or two leaves and bending them over the developing curds.

5 Apply a suitable insecticide to the soil around the plants to combat cabbage root fly. Continue to water the transplants daily until they are fully established. Make sure they are never short of water because otherwise they will produce small heads.

6 May (frame-raised plants) or July (plants sown outdoors in March to April). Water in a dressing of sulphate of ammonia at 1 oz per square yard before the curds start to form.

MINI-CAULIFLOWERS

People with home freezers may want to grow cauliflowers with small curds. Certain varieties of summer cauliflower such as 'Predominant' produce high yields of miniature curds at row spacings of 9 in, with 4 in between plants in the rows.

The seed is best space sown at these distances to provide a uniform crop to pick more or less at one time, but transplanted seedlings can also be grown. Not all varieties of summer cauliflower can be grown in this way, but for the freezer it is well worth selecting suitable varities.

Apart from spacing requirements, the culivation of mini-cauliflowers is as for summer cauliflowers.

7 In dry weather apply water a 4 gal per square yard each week. If this is not possible give a single application at the same rate, when the curds are forming or 2-3 weeks before the crop is due to mature, to improve quality and yield.

8 June to August/September. Cut the mature cauliflowers as needed. The curds are ready for harvesting when they are firm and well developed but not yet beginning to open.

Broccoli and calabrese

Sprouting broccoli

Purple and white sprouting broccoli, with small leafy flowerheads on short stalks, are hardy and extremely useful for cold areas and poor soils where cauliflowers do not thrive. They are also well worth growing for the pleasant flavour of their young, succulent "spears"

Sprouting broccoli matures from January to May, the earliest of the purple varieties being ready to pick in mid-January, or in mild seasons and areas before Christmas. The white varieties, which are usually considered to have a better flavour, do not crop until late February or March and are less prolific.

Cultivation details and the timing of sowing and planting are very similar to those for winter cauliflower. Spacings of 27 in between the rows and between plants in the rows make the best use of the ground, although in very rich soils plants should be given a wider spacing of 30 in by 30 in.

Harvesting

The spears are ready to cut when the small flowerheads are well formed but before the flowers have begun to open. Pick the central spear first, when it is about 4 in long, and continue picking the side-shoots which develop at the same size. If the plants are picked every few days they will continue to provide young spears over a period of two months. It is important to cut sprouting broccoli regularly, both to stimulate further young growth and the prevent flowering. If the flowering shoots are allowed to develop fully the production of side-shoots stops.

Calabrese (green sprouting broccoli)

Calabrese is similar to sprouting broccoli in growth but differs in having a fairly large, compact, central, green flowerhead surrounded by smaller flowerheads that develop once the central head has been cut. It is less hardy than the purple or white sprouting broccolis but has the advantages of a shorter growing season and a delicious asparagus-like flavour. Calabrese takes 12-14 weeks to reach maturity and is in season from August until October, although if the autumn is mild it may continue to crop until severe frost occurs. The general principles of brassica growing, including pest and disease controls, apply equally to calabrese although it will grow well in relatively poor soils.

Sowing The seed is sown thinly in April or May in prepared seedbeds and the young seedlings are transplanted to the vegetable plot in June or July to follow an earlier crop. If a succession is required, seed can also be sown in June and the seedlings planted out in August for cropping in late September and October. The seedlings should be planted in rows 18 in apart with 18 in between plants in the rows. Closer spacings of 12 in by 12 in may be used provided that ample water is available. This produces smaller spears that are ideal for freezing.

Harvesting

As the central flowerheads mature cut them for use and then water in a light dressing of $\frac{1}{2}$ oz per square yard of a balanced general fertilizer, such as a proprietary brand of Growmore, around the plants. This encourages the growth of side-shoots within 2-3 weeks and, as with sprouting broccoli, picking these every few days when they are about 4 in long will maintain a succession of spears until frosts intervene.

July onwards

4 Keep the plants free from weeds. In dry weather apply water at 4 gal per square yard each week or give 1 application at the same rate as the central head forms.

BROCCOLI (SPROUTING)
'Claret' (purple), 'White
Sprouting' (white).

**CALABRESE (HEADING
BROCCOLI)**
'Corvet', 'Green Comet',
'Romanesco', 'Trixie'.

June to July

1 Water the seedlings in the seedbed the day before transplanting. Lift the seedlings carefuly. Dip the roots in thiophanate-methyl.

2 Plant the seedlings at 18 in intervals in rows 18 in apart and water them in well. Check that they are firmly planted by gently tugging the uppermost leaves.

3 Apply a suitable insecticide to the soil around the plants to combat cabbage root fly. Water the transplants daily until fully established.

5 When the central heads mature cut them for use. Water in a dressing of ½ oz of a balanced general fertilizer, such as a proprietary brand of Growmore.

6 Cut the side-shoots of calabrese every few days as they mature to maintain a succession.

Kale

The dark green, crinkly leaves and shoots of kale can be eaten from November to April. As it is extremely hardy it is a most useful vegetable for winter use. Kale is often said to taste bitter, but if the small tender shoots and leaves are used instead of larger coarse foliage, the flavour is very pleasant. It often succeeds where other brassicas will not, because it is tolerant of club-root and cabbage root fly, and it will grow and crop reasonably well on poor soils. It also tolerates harsher climatic conditions than other brassicas. Some varieties, known as rape kales, such as 'Hungry Gap' should remain where they are sown until they mature and not be transplanted. Most other varieties, whether curly or plain-leaved, are grown in seedbeds and transplanted like other bassicas. Kale is planted out later than most vegetables, so space must be set aside for it when planning the vegetable plot. A quick-growing early crop can be taken from the same land.

Some types of kale are ornamental, with coloured decorative leaves. These can be grown in flower beds where they fill the dual purpose of an ornamental and food crop. Perennial kales can be grown but they are less use as a food crop.

TYPES OF KALE

Plain

Curly

Rape

1 April to May. Sow the seed thinly and ¾-1 in deep in a prepared bed. Space the drills 6 in apart.

2 Late June to early August. Transplant the seedlings into rows 18 in apart with 18 in between each plant.

3 Autumn. Earth up each plant to the base of the first leaf as protection against frost and wind.

CURLY
'Dwarf Green Curled', 'Pentland Brig'.

PLAIN
'Nero di Toscana'.

RAPE
'Hungry Gap'.

Cultivation

Although tolerant of poor soils, kale grows most satisfactorily in fertile conditions. Kale will grow in most soils, whether acid or alkaline. The soil must, however, be well-drained. The general rules for brassica cultivation (see page 50) should be followed and the site should be open. Less shelter is needed than for other brassicas, but in areas exposed to cold winter winds some protection will be repaid by better growth. As with Brussels sprouts, firm planting is important, particularly with the tall varieties, because the crop has to withstand winter winds.

The seed of varieties to be transplanted is sown in prepared seedbeds in April and May for planting out from late June to early August. The seedlings should be planted in rows 18 in apart with 18 in between the individual plants in the rows. For dwarf varieties the spacings should be 15 in either way. Early varieties sown in April are ready for picking in November and December, with later varieties continuing until the following April. 'Hungry Gap' and its relatives should be sown very thinly in drills 18 in apart and the young seedlings thinned by stages so that they are 18 in apart in the rows. Alternatively, 2-3 seeds can be sown at stations 18 in apart in the rows. Remove all but the strongest seedling at each station as soon as they can be easily handled. Their cultivation otherwise differs little from winter cabbage (see page 56). Perennial kales are usually propagated by cuttings from established plants.

As with cabbage, avoid nitrogen-rich fertilizers which encourage top growth and thus increase the risk of frost damage. Earth up around the stems to protect the plants from wind and frost. Kale shows some tolerance of club-root and cabbage root fly, but can be badly affected by aphids, which can be controlled by spraying with a systemic insecticide such as heptenophos or pirimicarb.

Harvesting

Kale should be used after the brassica crops have been harvested. It tastes best after frost. Use young leaves and shoots only, pulling off and discarding yellowing or tough old leaves. Further side-shoots will be produced, particularly with varieties such as 'Pentland Brig', and again these should be gathered when young and succulent. Pick the sideshoots from the top downwards. Some varieties produce edible flowering heads.

'Hungry Gap' Varieties

4 Winter to early spring. Harvest kale by picking the young shoots from the top of the plant downwards.

1 May. Sow 3 seeds at 18 in intervals in their final growing position.

2 June. Thin the seedlings to the strongest at each station.

Spinach/New Zealand spinach

Spinach (*Spinacia oleracea*) is an annual plant. Highly nutritious, it is grown for the use of its leaves which are either cooked or eaten raw in salads. New Zealand spinach (*Tetragona tetragonioides*) is not botanically related to ordinary spinach but is also grown for its leaves. The roughly triangular, blunt-tipped leaves are milder in flavour than those of ordinary spinach.

Cultivation
Ordinary spinach needs a soil rich in organic content and therefore capable of retaining water. When winter digging, add well-rotted compost or manure.

Soil and situation Spinach will not thrive on poor, dry or extremely acid soils. It grows best at a pH of 6.5-7.5. Since it is very fast growing, summer spinach can be cultivated as a catch crop between rows of taller vegetables, such as peas or beans, which provide slight shade in the summer months.

Summer spinach
For a continual supply of fresh leaves throughout the summer, sow the seed at two or three week intervals from March to May. Take out 1/2-3/4 in drills, 12 in apart, and sow the seed very thinly.

Thinning Spinach has a much better flavour if it grows without any check and for this reason both thin sowing and early thinning are important tasks. Overcrowding in the row results in weak plants that run to seed easily. As soon as the seedlings have emerged and are large enough to handle, thin them until the individual plants are 3 in apart. As soon as these plants begin to close in on each other, thin again until they are 6 in apart. These thinnings can be eaten. Hoe between the rows very regularly to keep down weeds.

Watering Spinach must be kept well watered, especially in hot dry weather when there is a risk of bolting. Give the plants up to 4 gal per square yard each week in such conditions, even if they are still very small.

Winter spinach
Late-season sowings can be disappointing if round-seeded varieties are used. For the best results select a bolt-resistant variety of spinach such as 'Sigmaleaf'. Sow the seed in the usual way in late August or September but at this time it is best to choose a sunnier site. Cover the growing plants with cloches from October onwards in cold areas and use a Dutch hoe to remove any weeds around the cloches.

Harvesting
Summer spinach is ready to pick 8-10 weeks after sowing. Up to half the foliage on each plant can be picked at a time.

NEW ZEALAND SPINACH

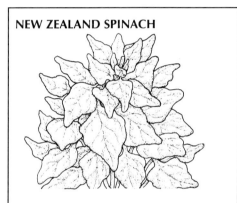

New Zealand spinach needs a good medium to light soil and an open sunny position. It is not a hardy plant and must be sown indoors in early March for planting out in May or as soon as the danger of frost is past. The seeds are very hard and it helps germination if they are soaked in water overnight before sowing. Sow three seeds together in a 1/2 in drill with 1 ft between each group of seeds. Thin the seedlings when they emerge, leaving the strongest one from each group of three. New Zealand spinach has a trailing habit and takes up a lot of ground. It does not bolt in hot dry weather although it should be watered well during such spells to encourage growth. Hoe regularly at first to keep down weeds, but later the plants' own thick growth will control them. Pinch out the tips of well-grown plants to produce more branching and young leaves for picking. From June to September harvest New Zealand spinach by picking a few leaves from each plant. Regular picking encourages them to keep on producing.

SPINACH
'Sigmaleaf' (spring or autumn sowing), 'Spokane' (spring sowing), 'Triathlon' (spring or autumn sowing), 'Trinidad' (spring sowing).

NEW ZEALAND SPINACH
No named varieties available.

Winter spinach takes longer to mature and is not ready until about 12 weeks after sowing. Only a few leaves should be taken from each plant at any one time.

Pick the outside leaves while they are young and tender by breaking the stalk by hand. Do not tear the leaf stems away from the plant's base because this damages the plant. If spinach is harvested regularly in this way the plants are encouraged to produce more leaves and the cropping period is longer.

Storing Spinach is best consumed as soon as possible after harvesting, although it can be frozen successfully.

Pests and diseases
Proper thinning of the growing plants and vigilant watering should deter downy mildew. But if it does strike, spray the plants with mancozeb.

Summer spinach

1 Winter. Incorporate well-rotted compost into the soil during winter digging.

2 March to July, every 2-3 weeks. Sow the seed thinly in 1/2-3/4 in deep drills, 12 in apart. Thin to 3 in apart.

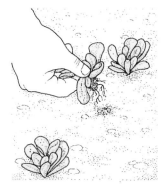

3 When the seedlings begin to touch each other, thin again to 6 in apart. These thinnings can be eaten.

4 In dry weather apply water at a rate of up to 4 gal per square yard each week. Hoe weeds regularly.

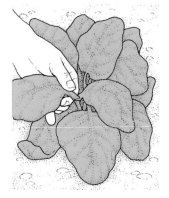

5 Eight to ten weeks after sowing, cut or pick the outside leaves by breaking away their stalks.

Winter spinach

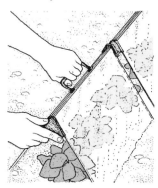

October onwards. In cold areas cover the growing plants with cloches.

Spinach beet/Seakale beet

Spinach beet is a biennial plant also known as perpetual spinach. It is grown for its leaves, which make an excellent substitute for ordinary spinach. It is less liable to bolt, has a heavier yield and withstands drought. Some people prefer spinach beet because its leaves are less acid than true spinach. The roots of spinach beet are not eaten.

Cultivation
Spinach beet does not need as rich a soil as ordinary spinach (see page 70) but if such soil is available it will thrive in it.
Soil and situation Prepare the seedbed in the same way as for ordinary spinach. Do not worry about providing slight shade, however, because spinach beet prefers a more open position and it does not have the same tendency to bolt in hot summer weather. Spinach beet is sown in April and then again in July. These two sowings should provide a continual supply of leaves during summer, autumn and winter.

Sow the seed in groups of three or four at about 9 in intervals in ½-¾ in drills which are 15 in apart. As soon as the seedlings have grown big enough to handle thin them,

leaving one strong seedling at each station (at 9 in intervals). Hoe between the rows and remove any flowerheads that develop. Water the plants regularly. In dry weather applications of up to 2-3 gal per square each week are beneficial.

Harvesting
Pick the leaves as soon as they reach a suitable size (usually at the end of May or early June from April sowings). Spinach beet continues to flourish if some of the largest leaves from each plant are picked before they become too coarse and tough. Pick them as near to the ground as possible. Even if some leaves from every plant cannot be eaten it is a good idea to pick them anyhow to encourage the production of more leaves. July sowings provide autumn and winter harvests. Spinach beet is quite hardy and it will tolerate average winter frosts.

Pests and diseases
Spinach beet is relatively trouble free, although virus problems can occur and proper thinning is an important factor to prevent downy mildew (see page 29).

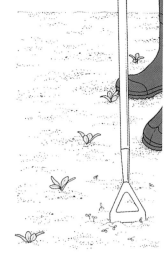

1 April or July. Sow 3-4 seeds at 9 in intervals in ½-¾ in deep drills, 15 in apart.

2 When the seedlings are big enough to handle thin the groups, leaving 1 seedling at each station.

3 During the growing season hoe between the rows regularly.

SPINACH BEET
No named varieties.available
sometimes known as
'perpetual spinach'.

SEAKALE BEET
'Fordhook Giant' (white mid-
ribs),
'Rhubarb Chard' (red mid-ribs).

SEAKALE BEET

Seakale beet is also known as Swiss chard or silver beet. A very attractive vegetable, it is a mutant of spinach beet with extra wide leaf stalks and midribs. The leaves are treated in the same way as ordinary spinach but the stalks and midribs may be used instead of seakale or asparagus. The midribs differ in texture from asparagus.

In April sow three seeds together at 15in intervals in ½-¾in deep drills that are 15 in apart. Thin the seedlings to the strongest in each group. Hoe regularly throughout the summer and water liberally, especially during dry weather. Sow again in July and give cloche protection in winter for greens the following spring.

Seakale beet is ready to pick from late July onwards or about four months after sowing. As soon as the leaves are big enough a few can be picked at a time from each plant. Break the stalks off at the base, taking the outside ones first. Once harvested seakale beet does not keep well and should be eaten immediately.

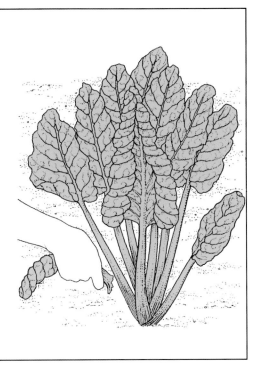

4 As they develop, water the growing plants liberally, up to 2-3 gal per week in dry weather.

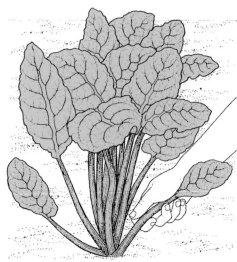

5 June onwards. Harvest a few of the largest leaves from each plant regularly, picking them off as close to the ground as possible. Pick regularly to encourage production.

Asparagus 1

Asparagus is a perennial fern-like plant grown for its young shoots which are cut as fat, succulent spears soon after they come through the soil. Appreciated as a luxury vegetable, asparagus is expensive to buy but economical to grow because the same plants, when established and well-managed, will provide crops for 20 years or even longer. Asparagus is easy to grow and it is a beautiful plant, but it does require time and patience.

Cultivation

Plants may be raised from seed but there is a long, three-year delay between seed sowing and the first crop. The more usual way of starting an asparagus bed is with bought crowns, which can be one, two or three years old. For all ages the period between planting and harvesting is the same. The one-year-old is the best buy because it is cheaper and it establishes a good root system as quickly after planting as does a two- or three-year-old. Order the crowns from the nursery well in advance and ask for delivery in April, which is the best planting time.

Soil and situation Asparagus will grow in most soils but a pH of 6.5-7.5 is preferable and good drainage and freedom from perennial weeds are essential. Dig a dressing of well-rotted manure or compost at 15 lb per square yard into the top spit in the autumn or early winter before planting. Asparagus roots tend to develop laterally so it is best to maintain the food supply in the top 12 in of soil. Asparagus grows best in an open site.

The first year

Never let the crowns dry out; choose a moist day for planting and leave the crowns wrapped until the last minute.

Planting The traditional asparagus bed, which consists of three rows of crowns with access on either side, is more than 5 ft wide. However, if only a single row is planted in each trench weed control and cutting are easier. In April dig a trench about 10 in deep and 15 in wide for each row. Then lightly fork in a balanced general fertilizer, such as a brand of Growmore, at 3 oz per square yard. In very nitrogen-rich soils dig in 1½ oz superphosphate

SOWING ASPARAGUS

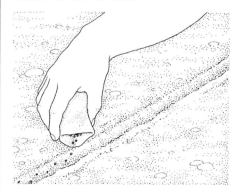

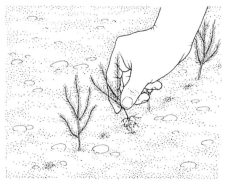

Asparagus seed can be sown outdoors in March or early April.

Sow the seed thinly in ½-¾ in deep drills, 18 in apart. When the seedlings emerge thin them until they are eventually 6 in apart. Keep the bed completely weed-free and water in dry weather. The seedlings can be transplanted to the permanent bed in March or April of the following year.

However, another year in the seedling row will mean that the seed-bearing female plants can be identified and removed before their seeds fall and germinate. In a permanent bed planted with male crowns only there is no seedhead production and constant weeding out of unwanted seedlings will not be necessary. Plant out and proceed as for one-year-old crowns.

The first year

1 Winter. Dig the ground 1 spit deep, incorporating well-rotted manure or compost with a fork and removing perennial weeds.

2 April. Dig a trench 15 in wide and 10 in deep. Lightly rake in fertilizer at 3 oz per square yard. Make a 3 in deep ridge at the bottom of the trench.

3 April. Plant the crowns at 18 in intervals on the ridge with the roots sloping outwards. Cover the crowns with 2-3 in of soil.

4 October. Cut the fern when it has turned yellow. Apply a 2-3 in layer of manure or compost and mound up the soil several inches deep over the row.

Asparagus 2

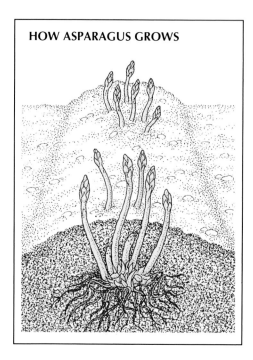

HOW ASPARAGUS GROWS

and 1 oz sulphate of potash. Make a ridge in the bottom of the trench and place each crown at 18 in intervals on the ridge, with the roots spread outwards over the ridge. Cover them quickly and carefully with fine soil to fill in the trench. If more than one trench is dug the rows should be 4 ft apart.

Once an asparagus bed is established its upkeep is routine. The common reasons for deterioration are lack of weeding, cutting over too long a season and disregard of the need for fern production. Hand weed regularly and never cultivate deeply or dig near a bed because asparagus roots spread out widely and are easily damaged. In the autumn when the foliage turns yellow, cut it down and clear any weeds. Mound up the soil several inches deep over the row.

The second year
In late February or early March top-dress with a balanced general fertilizer, such as Growmore, at 3 oz per square yard.

Do not cut the foliage until it yellows in the autumn. Then clear the bed and apply a

The second year

5 Late February to early March. Top-dress the bed with fertilizer at 3 oz per square yard.

6 Autumn. Cut down the yellow fern and apply manure or compost. Ridge up the row with soil if necessary.

2-3 in layer of well-rotted manure or compost. Ridge up the row with soil if necessary.

Harvesting
Do not cut any spears until the third season after planting. Eventual heavy cropping depends on a slow build-up of crown size, starting with the all important first two seasons, when no cutting should be done.

The cutting season for asparagus is from the end of April to late June, and no longer. Cut all the spears when they are 5-6 in above ground, even if they vary in thickness. In the third year cut for a period of six weeks after the first shoots appear. In the fourth and subsequent years the cutting period is up to eight weeks.

A special asparagus knife is ideal for cutting, but an ordinary sharp knife used carefully will do. By the time a bed is established the crowns will be about 4 in below the soil surface.

Cut the spears obliquely about 1-2 in below the soil surface. An asparagus crown produces many small shoots at different stages of maturity and it is important to cut the spears cleanly and carefully so that the plant will continue to crop.

Aftercare
From June onwards the ferns must be allowed to grow in order to play their vital role in building up food reserves in the crown for the following year's crop. To encourage this growth apply a general, balanced fertilizer at 3 oz per square yard immediately after the last cutting.

When the fern has turned yellow, and not before, cut it down to ground level. Burn it, because it is too woody for the compost heap. Clear away any debris and tidy the bed after cutting the fern down.

Pests and diseases
Hand remove adult asparagus beetles during the cutting season. Later use pyrethrum, derris or pirimiphos-methyl against the grubs on the leafy stems. If slugs are troublesome control them by the methods described in the section on pests and diseases (see page 33).

Third and subsequent years

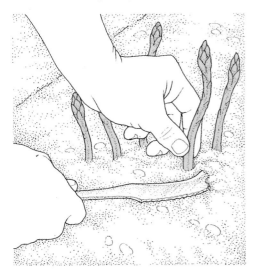

7 April to late June. Cut all the spears with a sharp knife when they are 5-6 in above soil level. Cut each spear obliquely 1-2 in below the soil surface.

8 June onwards. Immediately after the last cut, apply a general, balanced fertilizer, such as a brand of Growmore, at 3 oz per square yard to the bed.

Globe artichokes/Cardoons

The globe artichoke is a perennial plant grown for the attractive foliage and the immature flowerheads, parts of which are edible.

Cultivation

The globe artichoke is simple to cultivate but it takes up a lot of space for a small yield. It is a three-year crop, discarded after the third year. Globe artichokes can be grown from seed but some seedlings produce inferior flowerheads so they are usually grown from "suckers", the rooted offsets of established globe artichoke plants.

Soil and situation An open position and a fertile soil of pH 6.5-7.5 is required for the best results, although artichokes are tolerant of most soils unless the drainage is poor. Dig the ground well in winter, incorporating manure or compost, and a couple of weeks before planting rake in a general balanced fertilizer at 3 oz to the square yard.

Planting Take suckers from the base of established plants from March to April. The ideal sucker is sturdy, short-jointed and about 8-9 in long. Remove them close to the main stem, making sure that some root is still

The first year

1 March to April. Cut the suckers cleanly, with some root still attached, from the base of established plants.

2 Plant the suckers at 2 ft intervals in rows 2½ ft apart and water them. Keep watering until the plants are established, when the leaves stop flagging.

4 August to October. Cut unripened flowerheads before any of the bud scales are purple. In November cut old stems right down and cover the rows with straw.

The second year

5 March to April. Remove the straw from the rows and top-dress with 3 oz per square yard of a general, balanced fertilizer.

attached. Plant the suckers in permanent rows 2½ ft apart with 2 ft between individual plants. They should be watered initially until they are established and then during dry spells. Hoe weeds throughout the summer.

Harvesting
In the first year each plant will produce 4-6 flowerheads for cutting in August. In the second and third years each plant should produce 10-12 heads and cutting can commence in July. Cut when the heads are mature and fleshy but while the scales are still shut tight.

3 Throughout summer. Hoe regularly to keep the rows weed-free and water in dry weather.

6 July to October. Cut the mature fleshy flowerheads when the scales are still shut tight. Cut the main heads first, followed by the smaller heads.

If the scales open, revealing a purple tinge at the base, they will be unpalatable. Cut the main heads first, followed by the smaller side-heads.

Cut the old stems down after harvesting and tidy the rows. Cover the rows with straw or bracken. The plants are at their best when two or three years old, after which they should be discarded.

Pests and diseases
For precautions against blackfly and slugs see pages 31 and 33.

CARDOONS
Closely related to the globe artichoke, the cardoon is an attractive plant grown for the fleshy stems of its inner leaves, which require blanching.

Sow the seed in April in a well culti-vated, moist soil. Sow groups of 3-4 seeds at 18 in intervals in rows 2½ ft apart and thin to the sturdiest seedling at each sta-tion. From late August to early September blanch cardoons. After 4-5 weeks the stems should be ready to harvest. Lift whole plants up with a fork and trim off the roots. Cardoons are not fully frost hardy.

Blanch cardoons by wrapping the stems of each plant in a light-proof material such as black polythene. Loosely tie the cover-ing and hoe up soil around the base of each plant.

Seakale

Seakale is a hardy perennial plant, grown as a luxury vegetable for the production of its blanched leaf stems.

Cultivation

Seakale can be produced from seed but it takes two years to produce edible shoots. Most people prefer to use "planting crowns" which can be obtained from a nursery or another gardener, or produced from root-cuttings (thongs). Seakale blanched outdoors can be left to produce more crops, provided they are well tended, in the following years.

Soil and situation Seakale needs a well-drained fertile soil of pH 6.5-7.5; the best results are obtained in deep, rich sandy loams. An open site with no competition from other crops or nearby tree roots is also necessary. Dig the ground well in winter, incorporating 15 lb per square yard of well-rotted garden compost or manure.

In spring, 1-2 weeks before planting, rake 3 oz per square yard of a balanced general fertilizer, such as Growmore, into the soil.

PROPAGATION FROM ROOT-CUTTINGS

Take root-cuttings (thongs) from the fleshy side roots (off the main roots) of plants lifted in the autumn. They should be about 3-6 in long and as thick as a pencil. Make a straight cut across the top (the end nearest the main root) and a sloping one at the bottom to distinguish them for planting later. Store in sand until March.

1 Late March to early April. Plant the crowns, having rubbed off all but the strongest bud from each, 2 in deep at 15 in intervals in rows 18 in apart.

4 End of March to early April. Scrape soil away from the blanched crowns and cut off the shoots with a sharp knife when they are 5-7 in long.

5 End of April. Stop cutting and rake in 3 oz per square yard of a general balanced fertilizer. Mulch the bed with well-rotted compost or manure.

Planting In late March plant the crowns or "thongs" 2 in deep and 15 in apart with 18 in between the rows. Before planting rub off all but the strongest bud from each crown.

Keep the plants weed-free and water them in dry weather. Remove any flower stems.

Blanching In the autumn clean up the beds and cut down the yellowing foliage. In January force seakale outdoors by placing a light-proof plastic pot, 9 in diameter, on top of each crown. Cover the drainage holes and place straw over each pot.

Harvesting
At the end of March or early April begin to cut, when the blanched shoots are 5-7 in long, and continue until late April.

Aftercare At the end of April finish cutting the blanched shoots. Rake in 3 oz of fertilizer per square yard and mulch the beds with well-rotted compost or manure. Keep the beds weed-free and repeat the blanching process in the following January. A well-tended seakale bed will continue to produce for about five years.

2 Summer. Hoe weeds regularly and water in dry weather. Remove any flower stems that develop. In autumn clean up the bed and remove the yellowing foliage.

3 January. Completely cover the crowns with light-proof, 9 in dia., plastic pots. Cover the pots with straw.

INDOOR BLANCHING

Seakale can be produced from November onwards by blanching indoors. Lift the crowns from late September to late October and trim off the side roots. Leave the main roots trimmed to a length of about 6 in. Then pot the crowns in plastic pots (9 in in diameter) filled with rich soil such as John Innes No. 3, allowing three crowns per pot. Cover each pot with another pot of the same size, placed upside down, and keep them in complete darkness at a temperature of 10°-13°C/50°-55°F. A cellar is ideal. The seakale should be ready within 5-6 weeks. Forced roots are useless for propagation so they should be discarded and burnt afterwards.

Celery

Celery is a biennial plant grown for its blanched stalks which are cooked or used for salads. There are white, pink and red varieties, the white producing the finest quality celery. The red varieties are the hardiest and they will stay in good condition well into the autumn months.

Cultivation

Choose an open site with rich, well-drained soil of pH 6.5-7.5. There are two methods of growing celery. By tradition it is grown in trenches which are gradually filled in to blanch the stems. Alternatively, self-blanching varieties can be used which do not require earthing-up but these are less hardy (with a correspondingly shorter growing season) than the trenched varieties. They require much less work and are especially suitable for heavy soils which are laborious to trench and where the trench may become waterlogged with consequent slug damage and rotting.

Trench method Take out a trench 15 in wide and 12 in deep in March or April. If more than one trench is required the centres of each should be 4 ft apart. Fork manure into the bottom of the trench at a rate of 15 lb (1 bucketful) per square yard and return the soil to within 3 in of ground level. The trench should then be left open until planting out time in early summer.

Sowing Use thiram-treated seed if available. In March or April sow the seed thinly in trays in John Innes seed compost or an equivalent, at 13°-16°C/55°-60°F. Do not cover the seed and keep it moist. The seed germinates 2-3 weeks. Prick out the seedlings when they have two true leaves into boxes of John Innes No. 1 or an equivalent potting compost, spacing them about 2½ in apart. Alternatively, place them singly in 3 in pots. Harden off gradually for planting out in late May or June. Just before planting rake in a balanced general fertilizer at 2-3 oz per square yard into the bottom of the trench and apply lindane or pirimiphos-methyl dust to combat carrot fly.

Planting In late May or June plant out the seedlings at 9 in intervals in double-staggered rows 9 in apart in each trench. Water the plants thoroughly. When the plants are about 12 in high cut out any side-shoots at the base and loosely tie the stalks just below the leaves, using raffia or soft string.

As with all leafy crops ample water is essential during the growing season. In dry weather apply 4 gal per square yard. Alternatively, 10-20 days before the final earthing up apply 4 gal per square yard. This improves the quality and size of the crop markedly.

Earthing up As the plants grow, earth up progressively at intervals of about three weeks, leaving plenty of leaf above the soil and taking

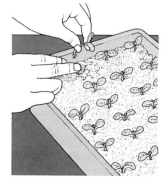

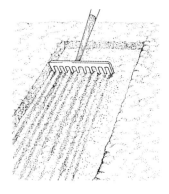

1 March or April. Dig a trench 15 in wide and 12 in deep. Fork manure into the bottom and return the soil to within 3 in of ground level.

2 March or April. Sow the seed thinly in seed compost at 13°-16°C/55°-60°F. Do not cover and keep moist. After 2-3 weeks prick the seedlings out and gradually harden off.

3 Just before planting, rake fertilizer into the trench bottom at 2-3 oz per square yard. Apply insecticides against carrot fly.

care not to let soil fall into the hearts. Earth up after rain when the soil is damp, never when it is dry, because the foliage acts as an umbrella and keeps the soil around the roots as dry or as damp as it was when earthed up, for a considerable time afterwards.

Harvesting
From October to February, depending on type and variety, lift celery carefully with a trowel as required. The roots may penetrate very deeply and in such cases it is best to lift with a fork. Bracken or straw placed over the trench assists lifting in frosty weather.

Pests and diseases
Celery leaf miner larvae bore into foliage leaving brown blisters. Pinch out affected leaves and spray with malathion at the first sign of damage. Slugs may be a problem, especially on heavy soils, and so put down slug pellets around the plants. Carrot fly attacks the roots of celery and should be combated by applying insecticide granules before transplanting. See page 32.

Celery leaf spot can be prevented by using bordeaux mixture or spraying the plants with carbendazim as soon as any spots are visible on the leaves.

SELF-BLANCHING CELERY

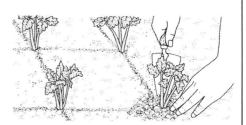

Sow the seed as for trench-grown varieties but plant out the seedlings on the flat. Prepare the bed in April by digging in well-rotted manure or compost at 15 lb per square yard. Plant out the seedlings during May in a square, not in a row, 11 in apart each way or 6 in each way for a higher yield of smaller sticks.

4 Late May or June. Plant out the seedlings at 9 in intervals in double-staggered rows 9 in apart. Water well.

5 July. When the plants are 12 in high loosely tie the stalks just below the leaves. Earth up every 3 weeks when the soil is damp to cover the leaf bases.

6 October to February. Lift celery carefully with a trowel or a fork. Place bracken or straw over the trench in frosty weather.

Bean sprouts/Alfalfa

The mung bean or black gram (*Phaseolus mungo*) cannot be grown as an outdoor crop in Britain because it requires tropical or sub-tropical conditions. However, it can be successfully germinated indoors to produce bean sprouts. These can be eaten raw in salads or cooked and they are a valuable source of protein and vitamin C. Bean sprouts are simple and quick to grow, and they can be "harvested" all the year round.

Cultivation

The beans can be sprouted at any time of the year provided they have sufficient warmth and moisture. Light must be excluded to blanch the shoots, keeping them sweet, white and palatable.

Sowing First rinse the beans and leave them to soak in cold water for 1-2 days or until they are slightly swollen and the skins have begun to split. Line a tray, shallow bowl or other suitable container with absorbent material: flannel, towelling, cotton wool or kitchen paper. Moisten it well and spread the soaked beans evenly over the surface.

Place the container in a polythene bag or wrap it loosely in polythene to provide insulation and help to retain the moisture. Do not make the bag airtight because this encourages rotting.

Keep the container in a warm place (16°C-24°C/60°-75°F) and exclude light by covering it with brown paper or newspaper or, alternatively, by placing it in a dark cupboard – an airing cupboard is ideal.

Watering The beans should be kept constantly damp, so water them 2-3 times daily. However, do not allow them to become too wet or too warm or they will go mouldy.

Harvesting

The sprouts are ready to harvest in 4-9 days depending on the temperature at which they have been grown. They should be 1½-2 in long, plump and white, with pale green leaves. Do not allow them to grow longer than this because they will become stringy and bitter.

Cut the bean sprouts with scissors or pull them up by hand. Remove the remains of the seedcoats if necessary.

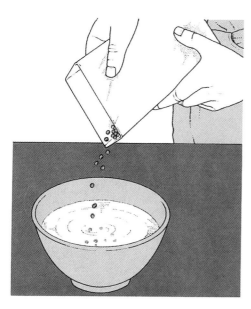

1 Soak the beans in cold water for 1-2 days or until the skins begin to split.

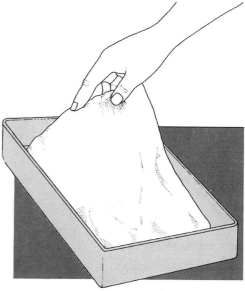

2 Line a shallow tray with absorbent material. Moisten well and sprinkle the soaked beans evenly over the surface.

ALFALFA

Alfalfa is grown commercially as a fodder crop but the seeds can be germinated indoors at any time of the year to produce shoots for eating raw in salads. They resemble cress in appearance and uncooked garden peas in taste. Sprouting is usually done by the "jar" method.

Put ¼oz of the seed into a jam jar or other similar clear glass jar. Cover it with water and leave it to soak overnight.

Seal the jar with a piece of muslin fastened with a rubber band. Pour off the water through the muslin, fill the jar with fresh water and pour off again. Rinse the seed daily in this way. Keep the jar at room temperature (20°C/68°F) and in the light but out of direct sunlight.

The shoots are ready to harvest in 5-7 days, when they have almost filled the jar and are a mass of curly white stems and bright green leaves. Pull them apart in tufts to use as required.

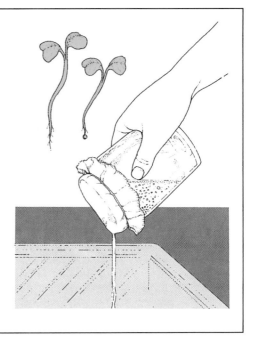

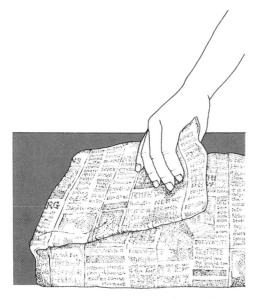

3 Place the tray in a polythene bag and cover with newspaper. Keep in a warm, dark place and water two or three times per day.

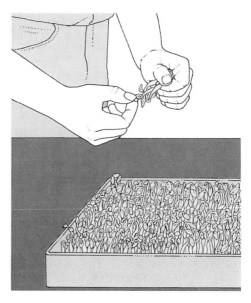

4 In 4-9 days, pull up or cut with scissors when the shoots are 1½-2 in long, plump and white. Remove any seedcoat remains.

Rhubarb

Rhubarb (*Rheum rhaponticum*) is a hardy perennial grown for its delicately-flavoured pink leaf-stalks or sticks, and is therefore classed as a vegetable not a fruit. The leaves contain oxalic acid and are poisonous. Rhubarb is in season from March to July, although earlier crops can be obtained in January and February by forcing plants.

Cultivation

Rhubarb grows best on a sunny site in a fairly heavy, acid soil of pH 5.0-6.0. However, it will tolerate a wide range of conditions and is likely to fail only on very waterlogged soils. The plants will stand for about 5-10 years, so the bed should be thoroughly prepared in the autumn before planting.

Dig the ground deeply, removing all perennial weeds and incorporating organic manure or well-rotted garden compost at a rate of 20-30 lb per square yard. Just before planting rake in a dressing of 3-4 oz of fertilizer.

Propagation Raising rhubarb from seed is a lengthy process which often gives poor results, so either propagate it from root division or obtain offsets of a named variety from a nursery. Propagation should be from established plants at least three years old. Cut the roots into offsets or sets with a spade or knife making sure each set has a bud.

Planting Plant in October to November or February to March, leaving 3 ft between the plants. If more than one row is required, leave 3-4 ft between the rows. The buds should be just below the soil surface. Firm in and water if necessary during dry weather. Cut out flowering shoots as they appear.

Harvesting

Rhubarb can be harvested from March to July. Do not pull at all in the first year after planting and only lightly in the second. Hold the stick near the base and pull up with a twisting movement. Take a few sticks from each crown as required, but always leave 3-4 leaves on each plant to avoid weakening it.

Aftercare In autumn, when harvesting is over and the foliage has died down, clean up around the plants and apply a light top dressing of a balanced general fertilizer at 2-3 oz per square yard. In late winter mulch with well-rotted compost or manure.

Pests and diseases

Stem and bulb eelworm may attack rhubarb, causing poor growth and distorted leaves. Crown rot is the only major disease, the symptoms of which are dull foliage, small sticks and dead buds. There is no cure for either of these problems so dig up and burn affected plants. Do not replant rhubarb on the same ground.

First year

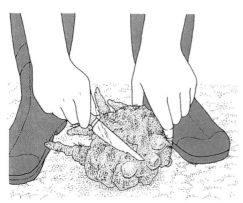

1 October to November or February to March. Cut the roots of an established plant into sets, ensuring each has at least 1 bud.

2 Plant the sets 3 ft apart in well-prepared ground, with the buds just below the soil surface. Rows should be 3-4 ft apart.

FORCING RHUBARB

 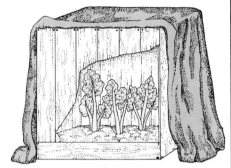

Forcing the plants during the winter produces earlier crops of pinker, more tender rhubarb. It can be harvested from February to March if forced *in situ* or as early as January if forced indoors.

Outdoors In mid-January to February cover the plants to be forced with a dustbin, bucket or barrel to exclude the light. Put straw or strawy manure over and around the cover for insulation. The plants should not normally need watering and the sticks will be ready in 5-6 weeks. Do not pick from the plants for at least two years after forcing.

Indoors In October to early November dig up strong clumps and leave them on the soil surface exposed to frosty weather for 1-2 weeks. This encourages rapid growth during forcing. Then pack the roots closely together in a box, cover with a thin layer of soil and water well. Invert another box and place it on top, and exclude light with newspaper or black polythene. Keep in a warm greenhouse or shed at 10°-13°C/50°-55°F. Water the plants occasionally to keep them moist. Pull the sticks in 4-5 weeks. discard the plants after forcing indoors.

Second and subsequent years

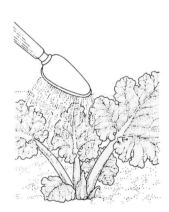  

3 Summer. Water the plants in dry weather and cut out any flowering shoots.

4 October. Remove old foliage. Apply 2-3 oz of fertilizer to each plant.

5 March to July. Pull sticks by grasping near the base and twisting upwards.

Haricot and soya beans

Haricot and Soya beans

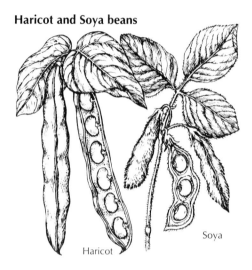

Haricot

Soya

The soya bean has a bushy habit and produces oval seeds that can be eaten whole with the pod, or shelled out and dried. It is a half-hardy annual, and warm weather is needed to ripen the pods and beans. Soya beans are the most protein-rich legume in the world but they are difficult to grow successfully in Britain. Haricot beans are the dried seeds of certain varieties of French beans.

Cultivation

Soya beans grow best in well-drained, fertile soils and warm, sunny situations. They do not thrive in cold, wet soils so delay sowing until the ground is warm and dry. Make sure that the soil is not acid; neutral soil (pH of 7.0) is ideal. Apply 1-2 oz per square yard of a general, balanced fertilizer such as Growmore and cultivate it in one or two weeks

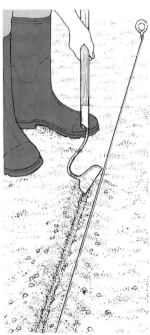

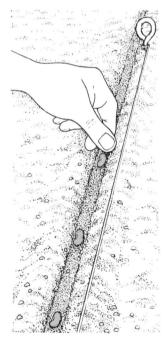

1 April. Using a draw hoe, take out 2 in deep drills in rows 18 in apart. Water the bottoms of the drills before sowing, and add a balanced fertilizer.

2 Early May. When the soil is warming up sow individual seeds at 2-4 in intervals.

3 During summer. Mulch the growing plants. Water when the flowers appear. Hoe around the plants regularly to eliminate weeds.

before sowing. No more fertilizer should be needed.

Sowing Sow in drills 2 in deep during May when the soil is warm. Never sow into cold, wet soil. Space the seeds 2-4 in apart in the row and leave 18 in between the rows. Water the bottom of the drill before sowing to provide sufficient moisture for germination. Mice may dig up and eat the seeds but they can be deterred by setting traps along the rows.

Growing Hoe around the plants to eliminate weeds, especially in the early stages. A mulch of peat, compost or straw will keep down later weeds and maintain a warm soil and reduce moisture loss. Water the plants regularly in dry weather.

Harvesting

Soya bean pods can be picked green and eaten whole. Alternatively, like haricot beans, they can be left to dry and the beans shelled out. In a fine autumn the pods may yellow and dry on the plant, but usually it is necessary to pull up the plants and hang them in a dry place. If the pods become damp they are likely to rot or develop mildew.

Pests and diseases

Aphids and red spider mites may attack the plants (see pages 31 and 32). Halo blight is difficult to control and infected plants should be burnt. Maturing pods and beans may be damaged by grey mould or mildews in wet weather. Spray with a suitable fungicide (see page 28).

Storing Shell the beans from the dried pods. Spread them on newspaper in a cool room to complete the drying. Store in a mesh bag.

4 Early autumn. When the pods turn yellow, pull up the plants on a fine day when both the foliage and the pods are dry. In wet weather it may be necessary to pull up the plants and hang them up to dry in the shed or cellar.

HALO BLIGHT

Halo blight is a bacterial disease that causes dark, water-soaked areas on leaves and pods; the characteristic "halo" forms as a yellow edge around the dark areas. Damp, humid conditions favour the spread of halo blight, which usually originates from infected seed. Never save seed for next season from diseased plants. Dig up and burn any plants with halo blight. Fungicidal sprays are usually ineffective against bacterial diseases.

French beans 1

French beans are half-hardy annuals. Dwarf and climbing types are available. They grow best in warm conditions. Early beans can be obtained from plants grown in heated greenhouses or under cloches. The beans are eaten with the pods, which are usually sliced. Green podded types with either flat or cylindrical pods are most common, and there are also yellow, wax-pod varieties. French beans are sometimes known as string beans or kidney beans. Haricot beans, which are the dried seeds of certain varieties of French beans, are dealt with on page 88. Like other beans, French beans are valuable for their vitamin and mineral content.

Cultivation

French beans grow best in a well-drained, fertile soil of pH 6.5-7.0. A layer of farmyard manure or compost dug in during the winter is sufficient to maintain fertility in most soils. Do not grow French beans in shaded situations. Apply, and work in, a fertilizer such as a proprietary brand of Growmore, at 1-2 oz per square yard a couple of weeks before sowing. Over-rich soils and too much nitrogenous fertilizer encourage soft growth and excessive leaf production. No top dressing should be needed for this crop.

Sowing Do not make outdoor sowings too early. A soil temperature of at least 10°C/50°F is needed for successful and rapid germination. Under good conditions, 75 per cent of the seed should germinate. French beans do not thrive in cold soils and the seeds will rot if conditions are too wet. Raise the soil temperature for early sowings and in cold seasons by placing cloches over the soil 3-4 weeks before sowing. The first dwarf bean sowings can be made outside in early May in most areas. Monthly sowings until July give beans throughout the summer. A late July sowing is often useful in southern districts in Britain, but the plants must be cloched in late

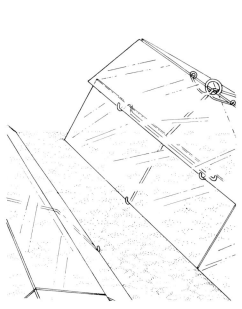

1 April. Place cloches over the seedbed to warm up the soil for early sowings.

2 Late April. Rake in general balanced fertilizer at 1-2 oz per square yard 1-2 weeks before sowing.

CLIMBING
'Blue Lake', 'Kentucky Blue',
'Purple Podded'.

DWARF
'Borlotta Firetongue',
'Golddukat', 'Masterpiece',
'Purple Teepee', 'Safari', 'Sprite',
'The Prince'.

GROWING UNDER CLOCHES

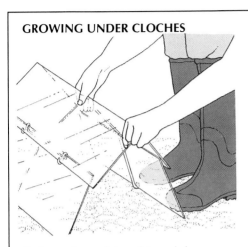

Early sowings of dwarf French beans can be made under cloches at the beginning of April. Put the cloches over the ground for 3-4 weeks before sowing in order to warm up the soil. Picking from early, cloched crops should begin in late June.

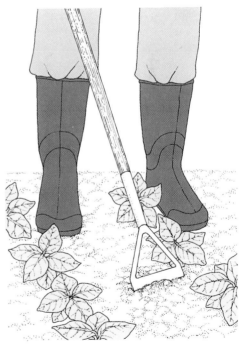

3 Early May. Sow individual seeds at 2-3 in intervals in 2 in drills, 18 in apart for dwarf, 3-4 in intervals and 2 ft apart for climbing.

4 Throughout summer. Hoe to keep down weeds and then mulch with peat, straw or black polythene to preserve moisture.

French beans 2

September to produce beans in October. Climbing types should be sown in early May.

Sow dwarf beans in rows 18 in apart. Space the seeds 2-3 in apart in 2 in drills. Water the bottom of the drill before sowing to encourage germination. Climbing beans are sown in the same way but with a 2 ft gap between the rows and the seeds 3-4 in apart.

Greenhouse and early cloched beans Very early pickings are possible from dwarf beans grown in a heated greenhouse from an early February sowing. Sow four or five seeds round the edge of a 9 in pot filled with John Innes No.2 or an equivalent compost. Pre-germinate or chit the seeds by keeping them on moist kitchen towelling in a warm place before sowing. Maintain a temperature of 15°C/60°F and keep the plants well watered once the flowers appear. Ventilate the greenhouse in warm weather to maintain sturdy plant growth. Picking should take place in May.

Cloches can be used to bring forward outdoor sowings of dwarf beans. a sowing can be planned for early April under cloches or polythene tunnels, but stand them on the site for three or four weeks beforehand to warm up and dry the soil.

Growing Climbing types need a support and training system. The plants will grow to 6-7 ft and canes, posts or strings on a post and wire framekwork all give good support. Stretch the strings at 4 in intervals between top and bottom wires and, if necessary, let two beans climb each string. Canes or poles should also be spaced 4 in apart.

Hoe out any weeds and mulch the plants in June with peat, straw or lengths of black polythene. Once the seedlings are established, do not water until the flowers appear unless the weather is dry. Too much water during early growth encourages leaves to grow at the expense of the flowers.

Water the plants generously once the flowers appear; beans are particularly sensi-

5 As flowers appear, carefully apply water at a rate of 3-4 gal per week. Avoid splashing the foliage.

6 July onwards. Pick the pods when they are 5-6 in long. They should snap in half easily and show no stringiness.

tive to moisture-stress at the flower opening and pod swelling stages and it is essential to keep them well watered at these times.

Applications of 3-4 gal per square yard each week markedly increases pod-set, yield and quality. Syringing the flowers to "set" the pods, a traditional practice, is not effective. Organic matter dug in during the winter will help to retain moisture.

Harvesting

Regular picking is essential to maintain a continuous supply of beans. Dwarf beans produce their pods over a relatively short period (hence the successive sowings) but climbing types continue to crop throughout the summer. Pick the beans while they are young and tender. Over-mature pods are stringy and show the beans bulging out the pod walls. Remove the pods carefully so as not to damage the plants; they should snap off the plants cleanly.

Pests and diseases

Aphids (green and black) may feed on the growing shoots, and red spider mites may be found on the under surfaces of leaves. These mites produce yellow dots on the upper surfaces of leaves, which eventually become bronzed and brittle (see pages 30-33). Grey mould (*Botrytis cinerea*) can be a problem during wet weather in the picking season. Damaged pods are soon infected and rot on the plant. Spray regularly with fungicide (see page 28) during wet or humid conditions.

The bacterial disease, halo blight, may attack French beans (see page 89). It causes dark, water-soaked areas on leaves and pods, and the characteristic "halo" forms a yellow edge around the dark areas. Damp, humid conditions favour the spread of halo blight and fungicidal sprays are usually ineffective against it. Destroy any French beans affected by the disease and never save seed for the next year from them.

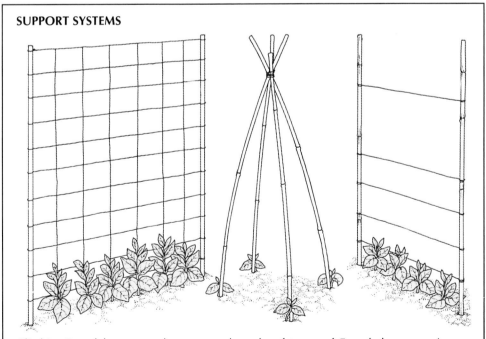

SUPPORT SYSTEMS

Climbing French beans must be supported on strings, canes or nets supported by poles and will grow 6-7 ft tall. However, dwarf types of French bean require no support and have a bushy habit with a height of approximately 18 in.

Runner beans 1

Runner beans are perennials that produce small root tubers, but they are usually grown as half-hardy annuals. In temperate zones they may be damaged by frost at the beginning or at the end of the season. The plants are very attractive with different varieties having white, pink or, more usually, scarlet flowers. Their tall habit and dense foliage make them a useful screen plant. A runner bean wigwam makes an attractive centrepiece in an annual flower border.

Cultivation

Runner beans should not be growing while frost is still a danger. When they are sown or planted rapid growth is required, however, and light, well-drained, fertile soils of pH 6.0-7.0 are best suited for this crop. Wet soils cause the large seeds to rot. Careful soil preparation for runner beans is rewarded with excellent growth and yields. Prepare a 2 ft wide, single spade depth trench in early spring. Fork large quantities of farmyard manure or well-rotted garden compost into the bottom of the trench before replacing the soil. These materials retain moisture during the life of the crop and encourage good growth and setting.

Situation Choose a sheltered but open, sunny site for runner beans, because winds can damage the plants and young beans. Still conditions also encourage the insects which are essential for runner bean pollination. One or two weeks before sowing, hoe in 2-3 oz per square yard of a general fertilizer such as a proprietary brand of Growmore.

Plant establishment There are several possible support systems for runner beans and the method of propagation varies with the system. Beans may either be sown or planted. Plants are raised in a cool greenhouse (10°C/50°F) in individual containers. Sow the seed approximately four weeks before the expected planting date. Pre-germinate or chit the seeds first between layers of moistened kitchen towelling kept in a warm place. A germination rate of more than 80 per cent can be expected. Keep the propagation temperature down to maintain strong, sturdy growth. Harden off the plants in a cold frame or under cloches for a few days before planting. Do not plant out until all danger of frost

EARLY CROPS

Early crops can be produced from transplanted plants raised by sowing seeds in pots in a cool greenhouse. Sow the seeds about four weeks before the expected planting date, which must be after the last frost. Make a good-sized hole with a trowel and plant a single bean plant beside each cane, pole or string. Sufficiently long shoots should be twisted around their support and the plants must be thoroughly watered at the base.

1 Early spring. Take out a trench one spit deep and 2 ft wide. Dig a generous supply of farmyard manure or well-rotted garden compost into the bottom and re-fill with the original soil.

CLIMBING
'Best Of All', 'Enorma',
'Pickwick', 'Polestar', 'Scarlet
Emperor'.

DWARF
'Hammond's Dwarf Scarlet'.

has passed. Sowing should take place outside from early May onwards depending on the frost incidence in the area. A soil temperature of at least 10°C/50°F is needed for germination. Cloches can be used to protect sowings made in early areas during April. Use the cloches to warm up the soil for three or four weeks before sowing and sow a single row with the beans spaced 6 in apart. Runner bean seeds should be sown 2 in deep and the positioning in the row depends on the support system.

Support systems

Runner beans are usually grown up supports, although dwarf plants can be grown. 'Hammonds Dwarf Scarlet' is a semi-dwarf variety which needs no pinching, but other varieties can be dwarfed by pinching out their growing point when they are 12 in tall. Pinched or dwarf beans produce slightly earlier crops than supported plants, but the yield is lower and the pods may be soiled. Space the seeds 6 in apart in rows 24 in apart.

Supported beans can be trained up canes, poles, strings or nets. The plants will grow 8 ft tall, but they can be stopped by pinching out the growing point when they reach the top of the support. Single rows of beans can be grown up any of the supports mentioned. Seeds should be sown at 6 in intervals and the canes, poles or strings should be spaced 6 in apart. If nets are used they should be attached to wires stretched between vertical stakes.

Double row systems use 8 ft canes or poles which are crossed over and wired or tied together at the top to form an inverted V-shape. Sow the beans at 6 in intervals in the rows which should be 24 in apart. If poles are scarce or expensive, two plants can climb each support, but the yield will be reduced. Leave a 36 in path between double rows.

Canes or poles can also be made into wigwam support frameworks. Four to ten supports may be used. A 4-cane wigwam has canes at the corners of a 3 ft square. The canes or poles are wired or tied together at the top. In this case erect the wigwam and sow or plant the beans next to each cane or pole.

2 April. Rake in 2-3 oz per square yard of a balanced general fertilizer. Use cloches to warm the soil in cold seasons.

3 Early May. Sow individual seeds 6 in apart in 2 in deep drills. Two drills 24 in apart are sown for double row growing systems.

Runner beans 2

Growing Gently twist the plants anti-clock-wise around their supports to encourage them to climb. Water runner beans only when they are in flower or cropping. Too much water early on encourages leaf growth at the expense of flowers and beans. If the plants become short of water, flowers will drop off and pods fail to develop. Bulky organic manures dug in during the soil preparations help to retain moisture around the roots. Mulch around the plants to eliminate weeds and minimize moisture loss.

Runner beans are insect pollinated and so care is needed when using insecticides. Use pirimicarb for aphids, applying it in the evening when pollinating insects have finished working. Pinch out the growing points of dwarf or "pinched" beans at frequent intervals to keep the plants compact.

The first severe frost kills runner bean foliage, which can be cut down and composted if it is disease-free. Diseased foliage should be burned. Dig the small root tubers into the soil because they will add useful nitrogenous material. Clean and store the canes or poles for next season. nets and strings should be burned after one season, but plastic netting can be sterilized.

Harvesting

Picking of the cloched and pinched crops starts in July, with the supported crops coming in at the beginning of August. Careful and rigorous picking of dwarf or pinched crops keeps down the number of soil-splashed and bent beans. Harvesting from these crops continues for about three or four weeks.

Supported crops produce beans until the first severe frost kills the plants. Pick them regularly to maintain a continuity of production. At the height of the season, it is necessary to pick every other day.

Pests and diseases

Aphids and red spider mites are the major pests, and grey mould (*Botrytis cinerea*) and halo blight may be problems in wet or humid weather. See pages 93 and 29-32 for details of symptoms and treatment.

Supporting a double row

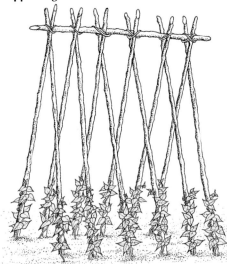

4 June. When the plants are 3-4 in tall erect a double row of crossed 8 ft poles. Space them 6-12 in apart, and train 1-2 plants up each. Place a horizontal pole on top for added stability.

5 June to July. Mulch around the plants once they are established. Use a 3-4 in layer of straw or peat.

SUPPORT SYSTEMS AND PINCHED BEANS

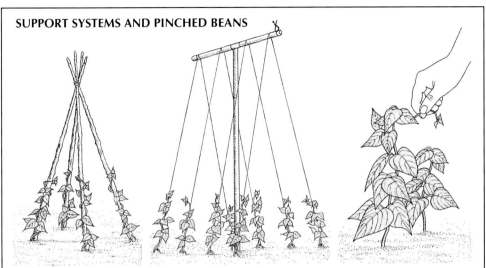

Strings, canes or poles are the most usual supports although nets are sometimes used. Plants may be grown in single or double rows. Wigwam supports are formed by joining 4-10 canes or poles together at the top. Unsupported plants – pinched beans – have the growing point removed to produce a dwarf habit.

6 June to July. Spray against aphids and red spider mites if necessary. Spray late in the evening to avoid harming pollinating insects, such as bees.

7 Late July to early August. Pick young, tender beans with no hint of swollen seeds through the pod wall. Regular picking, every other day if possible, encourages more runner bean pods to form.

Broad beans 1

Broad beans

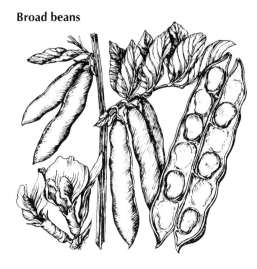

The broad bean is a hardy annual vegetable and the earliest maturing type of outdoor bean grown in Britain. The first pickings are made in June from over-wintered plants sown in the previous November. Special winter-hardy varieties are available today.

For picking from late June, sow under cloches in February. Successive spring sowings provide beans throughout the summer.

Cultivation

Broad beans – in common with other legumes – ideally prefer neutral or slightly alkaline soils, but grow well between pH 6.0-7.0. They tolerate relatively infertile soils but butter growth and heavier yields occur on rich, fertile, well-drained soils. Cold, wet soils must be avoided especially for the over-wintered crops. Broad beans have the largest seeds of

1 Early March. Take out drills 18 in apart and 3 in deep. Sow single seeds 5 in apart. For dwarf varieties make the drills 9 in apart and sow the seeds at 9 in intervals. Broad bean seeds are very large so there is no need to prepare a very fine seedbed for them.

2 April. Hammer stakes into the ground at each end of the rows, leaving 3-4 ft above the ground.

AUTUMN
'Aquadulce Claudia'.

SPRING
'Express', 'Imperial Green
Longpod', 'The Sutton' (dwarf),
'Verdy'.

all common vegetables and they will soon rot in waterlogged soils. Autumn-sown crops do not need fertilizer at sowing time. There should be sufficient remaining from the previous crop. Too much nitrogen at this time encourages soft growth, which is easily damaged by winter frosts. Rapid growth is required in the spring, however, and a top dressing of a nitrogenous fertilizer, such as 1-2 oz per square yard of nitro-chalk, should be applied as soon as growth recommences. Hoe the fertilizer in around the plants. Soil for spring sowings of broad beans should be given a dressing of 2-3 oz per square yard of a balanced general fertilizer, such as Growmore, 1-2 weeks before sowing. No more fertilizer should then be needed.

Sowing Over-wintered broad beans should be sown during the first half of November.

Use varieties recommended for over-wintering and aim to produce a strong 4 in tall plant to withstand the winter. Taller, softer plants will almost certainly be damaged or killed by frosts. Broad bean seeds are very large and there is no need to prepare a very fine seedbed. This is particularly true of over-wintered crops when the soil becomes compacted. Spring sowings of broad beans can begin outdoors as soon as the soil is workable, usually in February or March.

Unlike French and runner beans, broad beans will withstand some frost. The seeds germinate well at soil temperatures of 5°C/39°F. The germination rate should be at least 80 per cent. Successive sowings at monthly intervals will produce beans right into the autumn. Cloched broad bean crops can be sown in February.

3 April onwards. Hoe regularly around the plants and when they are big enough run string around the stakes at 12 in intervals to provide support as they develop.

4 When the plants are in full flower pinch out 4-6 in of shoot to reduce the danger of black bean aphids attacking and feeding on the young shoots in June, and to encourage a more uniform development of pods up the plants.

Broad beans 2

Single and double rows

Broad beans can be grown in either single or double rows. Research has shown that dwarf varieties should be sown 9 in apart with 9 in between rows. Taller varieties should be spaced 5 in apart with 18 in between rows. The seeds may be sown in a 3 in deep drill taken out with a draw hoe. Alternatively, they can be sown at the same depth in holes made with a trowel or dibber alongside a line.

The double row system, which produces the largest yield, is particularly good for cloched crops. Varieties with a dwarf habit, such as 'The Sutton', are also suitable for cloched growing.

Broad beans can also be sown in pots or boxes under glass in January and planted out in March. This system is useful in cold districts.

Hoe between over-wintered crops in the spring to incorporate the fertilizer top dressing and to aerate the soil. Hoeing for weed control is necessary until there is a good foliage cover of beans. Remove the cloches in April when the beans reach the glass. Taller varieties need not be supported. Stakes should be hammered in at the ends or corners of the rows. Leave 3-4 ft of stake above ground and wind successive lengths of string from the stakes all around the plants. Layers of string should be attached at 12 in intervals. Keep the plants well watered during flowering and cropping, but water only in dry spells at other times in the growing period.

Watch for black bean aphids (blackfly) which will attack the plants in June. They feed on the young shoot tips and their arrival usually coincides with the flowering of spring-sown beans. Remove 4-6 in of the growing

5 During flowering and cropping, water well to boost crop yield. Do not water before flowering unless the weather is very dry because too much watering during the early life of broad beans increases leafy growth at the expense of flowers and fruit.

6 June to July onwards. Pick young broad beans before the pod walls become tough and fibrous. Shell them from the pods before cooking – the attachment scars of individual seeds should be green rather than black.

tips to discourage this pest and to encourage more uniform development of pods up the plant. Spray plants with pirimicarb if aphids are present.

Harvesting

Picking begins in June and can continue, from successive spring sowings, into the autumn. Broad beans are usually shelled from the pods before cooking and the stage of picking is critical. The pods should not be tough and fibrous, while the beans themselves must be young and tender. Pods can also be picked when immature (4-6 in long).

After harvesting, cut off the plant tops and dig the roots in. Bean roots contain nitrogen-fixing bacteria which improve the soil fertility for subsequent crops. The roots also make excellent compost.

Pests and diseases

Blackfly can be sprayed with short-persistence insecticides such as heptenophos, pirimicarb or derris. Spray late in the evening to minimize damage to pollinating insects such as bees. Pea and bean weevils feed on leaves, producing a scalloped pattern round the edge. Nearly all broad bean crops develop dark brown spots or blotches on the leaves and stems, although the pods are attacked only in severe outbreaks. These are the symptoms of chocolate spot fungus (*Botrytis fabae*) related to grey mould (*Botrytis cinerea*). Poorly grown plants are attacked most severely, with damaged leaves, overcrowding and soft, lush growth contributing to the spread of the disease. Plants may become covered with rust late in the season (see pages 28-30).

7 After harvesting. Cut down the stems to within 4 in of the soil immediately after picking has finished. Compost healthy stem material and dig in the stem bases and roots.

AUTUMN-SOWN BROAD BEANS

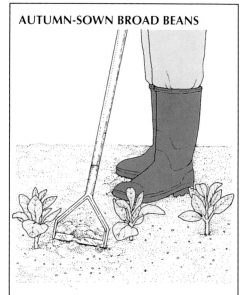

Sow broad beans in November in the usual way, using the special winter-hardy varieties available. Do not fertilize, or there will be too much growth which will suffer from winter frosts.

In February, apply a top-dressing of nitrogenous fertilizer, such as nitro-chalk, at a rate of 1-2 oz per square yard and hoe it in around the plants.

Garden peas 1

Peas

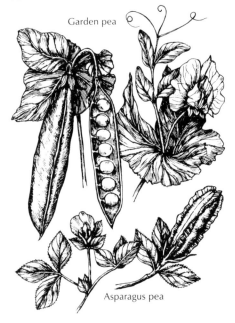

Garden pea

Asparagus pea

Peas are treated as hardy annuals, and the round-seeded types are the hardiest. These are sometimes sown outside in November to produce peas early the following summer. The wrinkle-seeded types are much less hardy and should not be sown until the spring. Sugar peas (mangetout) and the petit pois of France are closely related to garden peas. The yield depends upon the variety grown. Tall types produce two to three times as many peas as do dwarf types. Peas are usually shelled from the pods before cooking.

Cultivation

Peas must be grown on well-drained, rich, fertile soils of pH 6.0-7.0. Dig in a 2 in layer of farmyard manure or well-rotted garden compost in the winter to improve soil fertility and retain moisture. November sowings should be attempted only in sheltered districts and then only on freely-draining soils. Any hint of waterlogging will rot the seeds. Peas grown on well-manured soils do not require any fertilizers, but crops grown on low fertility soils respond to an application of 1-2 oz per square

Garden Peas

1 March until June. Use a draw hoe to make drills 2 in deep. Sow the seeds about 5 in apart in the bottom of the drill. For the distance between drills (18-48 in) check the mature height of the variety being grown.

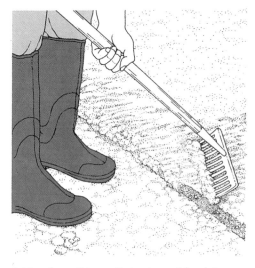

2 March until June. Rake the soil back into the drill after sowing. Firm the soil down on to the seeds by lightly tamping with the back of the rake.

PEAS
EARLIES
'Early Onward', 'Feltham First',
'Kelvedon Wonder', 'Little
Marvel'.

MAIN CROP
'Alderman', 'Hurst Green Shaft',
'Onward'.

**MANGETOUT
(SNOWPEAS/SNAP PEAS)**
'Oregon Sugar Pod' (snow pea),
'Sugar Gem' (snap pea), 'Sugar
Snap' (snap pea).

PETIT POIS
'Waverex'.

ASPARAGUS PEA
No named varieties available.

yard of a low nitrogen compound fertilizer. Incorporate the fertilizer just before sowing the peas. Fresh site each year recommended.
Sowing Peas are classified as first earlies, second earlies or main crop, according to the time taken from sowing until picking. First earlies take about 12 weeks; second earlies 13-14 weeks and main crop varieties 14-16 weeks. Successive sowings from the beginning of March until the end of April with these various maturity types produce peas from mid-June until August. Further sowings – until the end of June – can be picked until the end of September. A final sowing with the first early variety can be made in early July for picking in early October. It is necessary to cover these plants with cloches if early frosts occur. Cloches can also be used to protect very early sowings made in February. Use a first early, round-seeded variety such as 'Feltham First'. Picking should begin in early June. Seeds germinate at 5°C/39°F, but cold weather after germination and the resulting slow growth can lead to fungal and bacterial disease. Eighty per cent germination is normal. Dust the seeds with an animal repellent before sowing to deter mice.

Peas may be sown in single rows in a V-shaped drill or broadcast in an 8-10 in wide flat-bottomed drill. Experiments have shown that the best yields can be expected from lines of three drills 5 in apart, with 18 in between each group of drills. Space the peas 5 in apart in the drill, which should be 2 in deep. If sowing in a flat-bottomed drill, first make the drill with a broad-bladed draw hoe or with a spade. It should also be 2 in deep. Broadcast the seeds evenly in the drill so that they are about 3 in apart each way. Rake soil back into the drill and firm it lightly by tampering with the back of the rake. The distance between rows should be the same as the eventual height of the mature crops. This varies from 18 in for the dwarf, first early varieties to 4 ft for the later main crop types. These spaces can be used for catch crops of rapidly-maturing vegetables such as radishes early in the season. Birds may dig up the peas unless wire mesh guards are put over the rows of outdoor crops immediately after sowing.

Protecting from birds

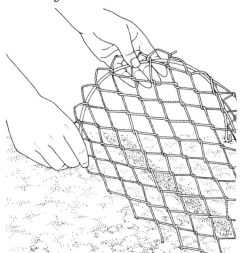

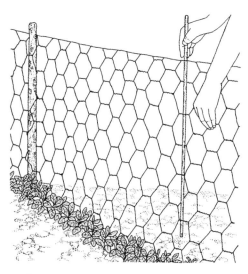

3 At the same time, put hoop-shaped, fine-meshed wire netting over the rows immediately after sowing to deter birds from digging up the seeds or eating newly emerged seedlings.

4 When the plants are 3-4 in tall erect the support system. Use a post and wire framework to support the netting up which the peas should climb.

Garden peas/Asparagus peas

Sugar peas and petit pois are sown in the same way but they reach heights of 4 ft and 3 ft respectively.

Growing Peas can be grown without supports but growth and yields are better if individual plants are able to climb and develop off the ground. The traditional method was to use pea sticks – twiggy pieces of hedge trimmings – pushed in alongside and within the rows. These sticks are now difficult to find and wire or nylon netting is more commonly used. Erect a post and wire framework along each row and attach an appropriate width of netting for the expected height of the peas. Put up the supports when the plants are 3-4 in tall.

Watering

Never allow peas to become too dry when they are in full bloom or when the pods are swelling. Too much water before flowering reduces the yield; water only in very dry spells. Mulching the plants with peat, straw or black polythene helps to reduce water loss and keep down weeds.

Harvesting

Picking of garden peas should begin about four weeks after full flower. Regular picking encourages more pods to develop. Pods at the base of the plant are ready first. The pods are the edible portion of sugar peas and it is vital that the peas inside them have not started to swell.

Petit pois must be harvested young or they lose their sweet, delicate flavour and become hard and unpalatable.

Cut down pea plants after harvesting and either put the roots on the compost heap or dig them into the soil, since their nitrogen content will improve its fertility.

Pests and diseases

Thrips (thunder flies) feed on the developing pods and give them a silvered appearance. Control with sprays of bifenthrin or pirimiphosmethyl. The major pest is pea moth. Eggs are laid in the flowers and the resulting larvae feed on the young peas in the developing pods. Crops flowering from mid-June to mid-August are most likely to be attacked. Spray

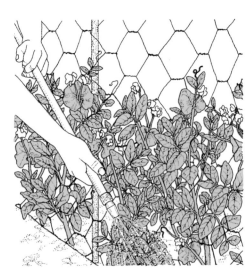

5 A week or 10 days after the first flowers appear spray with bifenthrin or pirimiphosmethyl to combat pea moth. Crops flowering from mid-June to mid-August are most likely to be attacked.

6 Mid-June to October. Pick young and tender but well-filled pods. Regular harvesting encourages more pods to develop.

with bifenthrin or pirimiphos-methyl, seven to ten days after flowering begins. Avoid the problem by growing varieties which flower outside the egg-laying period.

Asparagus peas

The asparagus or winged pea is quite different from other garden peas. It is half-hardy and has a bushy habit. The red flowers produce 4-winged fruits, 1-1½ in long, which are eaten whole. In some tropical countries asparagus peas are grown as a fodder crop, but in Britain they are unusual and little grown.

Cultivation

Choose a light, well-drained soil in a sunny position on which to grow asparagus peas. Apply 1-2 oz per square yard of a general, balanced fertilizer, such as a proprietary brand of Growmore, a couple of weeks before sowing or planting the crop.

Sowing Asparagus peas will be killed by frost, so choose a sowing date which takes this into account. Sow outside in early May when the main danger of frost is over. Space the seeds 4-6 in apart in 1 in deep drills, which should be 12 in apart. Water the bottom of the drill before sowing to encourage germination. Alternatively, the seeds can be sown in small pots in a cold greenhouse in early April and planted out at the end of May.

Growing Hoe weeds from around developing plants. Keep them well supplied with water from flowering time onwards. Too much water in the early stages reduces the yield. Asparagus pea plants have a tendency to sprawl and they should be supported by small sticks so as to avoid soiled or bent pods.

Harvesting

It is important to pick the fruits young, when about 1 in long, because they soon become tough and fibrous.

Pests and diseases

Asparagus peas can be vulnerable to the same pests and diseases as garden peas. Control thrips (thunder flies) if necessary, but there is no need to take the precautions against pea moth as advised for garden peas.

Asparagus peas

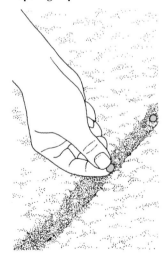  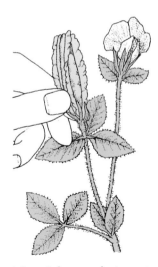

1 Early May. Sow the seed outside at 4-6 in intervals in the drill. In dry weather water the drill before sowing to aid germination.

2 When 2-3 in high, add stakes to support the plants.

3 Late July to early August. Pick asparagus peas when they are 1 in long, otherwise they soon become stringy and tough.

Sweetcorn

This half-hardy annual grows best in high temperatures and sunshine. Recently introduced varieties have made it a more suitable vegetable for temperate conditions. Male and female flowers are produced in different places on the same plant. Male flowers grow at the top of the plant whereas the female flowers – which develop into the sweetcorn cobs – are found lower down. Expect each plant to produce one or two cobs.

Sweetcorn plants

Cultivation

A light, well-drained and fertile soil of pH 5.5-7.0 is essential. Dig in a 2-3 in layer of bulky manure or garden compost during the winter. Avoid shaded sites but choose a sheltered position because the plants can be damaged by wind. Sweetcorn plants need plenty of food and water.

Apply 3-4 oz per square yard of a general fertilizer a couple of weeks before sowing or planting and be prepared to top-dress with 1-2 oz per square yard of nitro-chalk or a general liquid feed in June or July.

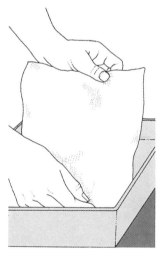

1 Winter. Dig a 2-3 in deep layer of manure or garden compost into the soil of a square plot.

2 April. Scatter seeds on to the surface of a layer of moistened tissue in a container. Place the closed container in a warm place.

3 Two or three days later, sow each seed in individual 3 in peat pots. Keep in a slightly heated greenhouse. Harden off the plants for 3-4 days before planting.

STANDARD VARIETIES
'Champ', 'First of All', 'Sunrise'.

SUPERSWEET VARIETIES
'Conquest', 'Dickson'.

BABY CORN
'Minipop', 'Minor'.

Sowing Early sowings can be made under cloches at the end of April provided the cloches have been used to warm up the soil beforehand. Outdoor sowings should not take place until mid-May, because a soil temperature of 10°-13°C/50°-55°F is needed for rapid germination. Sow in 1 in deep drills. Place groups of two or three seeds at intervals along the rows, which should be arranged in a block rather than a strip. A block of plants allows wind pollination to take place more readily. Space dwarf plants 12 in apart in each direction, and taller plants 15-18 in apart. Thin to one plant per station after the seedlings emerge. Protect the plants against birds with black cotton.

Better results are obtained with transplanted crops. Sow chitted (pre-germinated) seeds into individual containers or peat pots in a slightly heated greenhouse during April. Maintain a temperature of 13°C/55°F to produce plants for putting out in late May. Harden off the plants for 3-4 days in a cold frame before planting. Take care not to damage the roots, for a check suffered at transplanting reduces yields.

Growing Hoe to keep down weeds but be careful not to damage the young plant stems. Keep the plants moist if dry spells occur. No watering is normally needed until the flowers (tassels) appear, when regular weekly applications of 3-4 gal per square yard (unless the weather is very wet) will improve the quality and yield. In windy positions stake the plants, but raising the soil around the stems is usually sufficient to keep the plants upright.

Harvesting

Pollen is produced from the male flowers from mid-July onwards and falls on to the female flowers. These soon begin to wither, and the cobs should be ready about a month later. The cobs should be firm and well filled and are ready when the silks have turned nearly black. Test maturity by pushing a fingernail into one of the grains. A creamy liquid indicates that the cob is ready. Twist the cobs off the plant and cook or freeze them immediately.

Harvesting

4 Late May. Plant sweetcorn plants in a block 12-18 in apart each way (according to variety). Water regularly after the flowers appear.

5 August. When the silks have withered press a fingernail into one of the grains underneath the protective leaves on each cob.

6 If the pressed grain exudes a creamy-white liquid harvest the cobs with a twisting, downward movement away from the plant stem.

Onions 1

The onion is a biennial plant which is grown as an annual. The familiar bulbs are formed from swollen leaf bases. Salad onions (spring onions) are grown for the immature plants and should not produce bulbs.

Cultivation

Onions are easily grown from seed, and the bulb crop may also be grown from sets or be transplanted. Sowings can be made outdoors in February and March, or under glass in January, to mature in late summer and autumn. Sowings made outdoors in August and over-wintered are ready the following summer. Sets planted in March to April mature in August. Sow salad onions in the spring for summer and autumn use, and in July and August for use the following spring. Onion seed germinates very slowly and seedling growth is also slow.

Soil and situation The soil for onion growing should be well drained, reasonably fertile but not freshly manured. The pH should be more than 6.5. Choose a sunny but sheltered site. Soil-borne problems such as stem eelworm and white rot can be serious, so do not grow onions on the same ground each year.

Double dig the land in early winter, working a 2-3 in layer of bulky organic material into the lower spit. Leave the surface rough to allow it to break down naturally during the winter. Spring-sown and planted bulb onions (including sets) should be given a base fertilizer which contains about twice as much potash as nitrogen. Apply 2-3 oz per square yard of such a compound 7-10 days before sowing. Autumn-sown bulb onions do not require fertilizer at sowing time but give them a top dressing of 1-2 oz per square yard of nitrochalk in February.

Spring-sown crops

Onion seed germinates at temperatures of 7°C/45°F and above. In cold areas it is best to raise seedlings under glass. Sow in January for planting out in April. Sow in February under cloches, and in March in the open. The seedbed is most important. Digging in early winter should ensure that the soil is friable and breaks down easily. Work it down with a cultivator and rake it into a fine tilth, then make it firm and level. Be careful on silt or clay soils, where very fine tilths "cap" over if wet conditions are followed by drying

Spring-sown onions

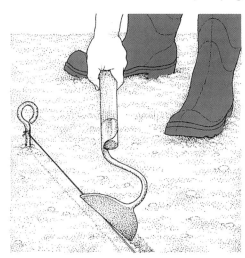

1 February to early March. Apply a balanced general fertilizer at a rate of 2-3 oz per square yard 7-10 days before sowing. Rake it in and tread the soil down to produce a firm seedbed with a fine tilth.

2 Late February to mid-March. Draw out drills 9-12 in apart and ½ in deep. Water the drills if the soil is dry. Sow the seed thinly.

ONIONS
AUTUMN-SOWN
'Buffalo'.

SPRING-SOWN
'Ailsa Craig', 'Albion',
'Bedfordshire Champion',
'Lancastrian', 'Red Baron'.

ONION SETS
'Balstora', 'Radar', 'Showmaster',
'Stuttgart Giant'.

PICKLING ONIONS
'Paris Silver Skin', 'The Queen'.

SALAD (SPRING) ONIONS
'Guardsman', 'Ishikura', 'White
Lisbon'.

weather (see page 15). Seedlings can find it difficult to penetrate the capped surface. Sow the seed thinly in drills 9-12 in apart and ½ in deep. Water the drill gently if the soil is dry. Thin to 2-3 in between seedlings as soon as they have straightened up.

During the summer onions should be kept free from weeds. Additional watering is not usually required except in very dry weather in spring or early summer when applications of 2 gal per 10 ft run may be given each week. Further feeding is unnecessary. As the bulbs approach maturity in mid to late August or September, their leaves begin to yellow and topple over. In wet seasons this may be delayed, and the tops should be bent over by hand to assist the ripening of the bulbs. The leaves of some plants in a row may remain standing and these bulbs often have a wide neck (bull necks). Do not attempt to keep these bulbs as they soon rot in store.

August-sown crops
Onions sown in autumn mature from late June to July, slightly earlier than crops sown in spring. The sowing dates for over-wintering varieties are fairly critical because it is import-ant to obtain young onions of a reasonable size to withstand the winter, but they should not be so large that they go to seed instead of forming bulbs when growth begins again the following spring. The seed should be sown during August or September in the same way as for spring-sown onions. Onion seed does not germinate well above 24°C/75°F, so in hot weather germination may be erratic. Pre-germination of the seeds at lower temper-atures or lowering the soil temperature of the seedbed by frequent light waterings may be necessary in some seasons. It is also useful to prepare the seedbed for August-sown onions about ten days before sowing. This cuts down attacks by bean seed fly which may be troublesome in freshly prepared seedbeds during summer.

If the seed has been sown thinly the young onions should be left to over-winter and thinned to 1½-2in (3 in for larger onions) in spring (March to April) as growth begins. A top dressing of 1-2 oz per square yard of nitro-chalk or a balanced general fertilizer should be gently hoed in around the young onions after thinning. Autumn-sown onions, particu-larly the Japanese varieties, should not be

3 April. As soon as the seedlings have straightened up thin them to 1-2 in apart, or 3 in apart if large onions are required. Treat the rows with pirimiphos-methyl or lindane dust against onion fly.

4 May to July. Keep the developing onions free from weeds. In very dry weather water at a rate of 2 gal per 10 ft run each week.

Onions 2

transplanted as transplants are liable to bolt.

Spring and summer cultivation is then as for spring-sown onions. Japanese varieties mature in late June, more traditional varieties such as 'Ailsa Craig' in July to August.

Less common onions

A number of other *Allium* species, grown mainly for their curiosity value or in the herb garden, are also excellent for eating and easily cultivated. The tree onion is a perennial plant which forms normal clumps of bulbs at ground level but also sends up tall tems bearing clusters of small onions instead of flowers. These may be used in cooking or to increase the stock by using them as sets. Easily grown on any well-drained soil, they provide crops for several years without complications.

The Welsh onion is also a perennial plant and it is a useful winter or spring substitute for the more conventional spring onions. The potato onion, which forms a number of mild-flavoured offsets just below soil level, can do duty for shallots. All are easily grown, providing useful and unusual space-fillers in a small garden.

Pests and diseases

Onion flies lay their eggs around the bases of young onion plants in late May. They hatch into larvae which tunnel into the developing bulbs, causing the whole plant to turn yellow and die. Young plants must be protected before the larvae attack. Treat the seedlings with pirimiphos-methyl or lindane dust. Stem eelworm causes twisting and thickening of the whole onion plant. Bulbs that become infested should not be stored. The pest remains in the soil from year to year, so rotate the onion bed around the vegetable garden (see page 38).

Downy mildew can be particularly bad in wet seasons. Grey patches appear on the leaves and turn purple as the disease progresses. Eventually the leaves topple over and collapse. Spay with mancozeb at the first sign of trouble. White rot is another soil-borne problem – this time a fungus. Onions and related crops are attacked. A grey-white growth appears on the basal roots and the leaves turn yellow. Dig up infected plants and do not grow onions on that soil again for 7-8 years. Neck rot may occur in storage (see page 29).

5 Late August to early September. If the leaves have not toppled over naturally by this time, which sometimes happens in wet weather, bend them over by hand to assist ripening.

6 September. Lift the bulbs for drying and storing when the fallen tops have begun to yellow and become brittle.

TRANSPLANTED ONIONS

 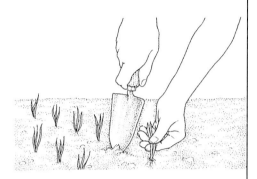

Early onions and those intended for showing should be transplanted. Sow the seed in trays during January in a heated greenhouse. Keep them at a temperature of 16°C/60°F. Germination is slow, but when the seedlings are large enough to handle they can be pricked out. For exhibition purposes grow each plant in a 3½ in pot containing a proprietary potting compost. For general garden purposes prick out the onion seedlings individually into peat pots or into a seed tray, spacing them 2 in apart each way.

Gradually reduce the greenhouse temperature to 10°C/50°F and harden off the plants in a cold frame or under a cloche for a few days before planting. Plant during early April in rows 12-15 in apart. Space the onions 2-3 in apart in the row. Plant shallowly with a trowel – deep planting hinders bulb development. Water thoroughly after planting.

Autumn-sown onions

 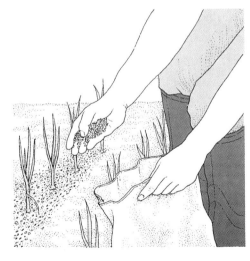

1 August to September. Prepare the ground and sow as for spring-sown onions, but do not thin the plants.

2 March to April. Thin the young plants to 1½-2 in apart, 3 in if large onions are required. Top-dress with 1-2 oz per square yard of balanced general fertilizer or nitro-chalk after thinning.

Onions 3

Onion sets

Sets are partly developed onion bulbs. They are stored during winter and replanted in the spring, when they grow away rapidly. Sets are particularly useful for growing onions in places with short growing season such as northern Britain. Consistently higher yields are possible from sets or bought-in plants. As the sets have to be bought, it is more expensive to grow onions this way. This expense can be avoided by saving some onions from the previous season. The best sets are ³/₄ in in diameter and firm. It is also sensible to choose sets of this size when purchasing them because they are less likely to bolt than larger bulbs and cheaper per plant.

Planting onion sets

Plant them in late March or early April into a fine tilth. Mark out rows 10 in apart with a garden line and push the sets into the ground at 2-3 intervals, or at 4 in intervals if larger bulbs are required. There is no point in using the wider spacings sometimes recommended because the yield from a given area will be much reduced. Only the nose of each bulb should be visible. Firm the soil around the sets.

Birds may pull up the sets and prolonged frosty weather may also lift them out of the ground. In either case, they should be replanted immediately.

The remaining cultural operations of watering, weed control and harvesting (see pages 108-110) are as for spring-sown or transplanted bulb onions.

SALAD ONIONS

Salad onions, or spring onions, are immature onion plants. They are grown close together and eaten as a salad vegetable when the bulb is ¹/₂-1in across. Many of their requirements are the same as for bulb onions. The earliest salad onions are ready in the spring from sowings made at the end of the previous August. Continuity through the summer is then maintained from successive sowings made at two-week intervals from mid-February until mid-June. Salad onions are grown close together in rows 4 in apart to prevent bulbs from developing. Sow the seed reasonably thinly in ¹/₂ in drills. The drills should be watered before sowing if the soil is dry. The plants should grow ¹/₂-1 in apart in the rows. Pull salad onions before the bases swell. It helps to water them before pulling from dry soils.

1 February to June, every 2 weeks make sowings in ¹/₂ in deep drills 4 in apart.

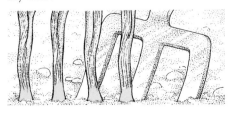

2 Summer. Lift the immature onions with a fork as the bases swell.

RIPENING AND STORAGE

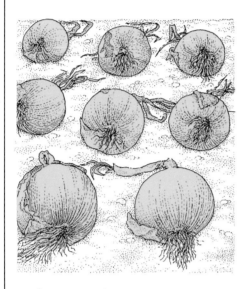

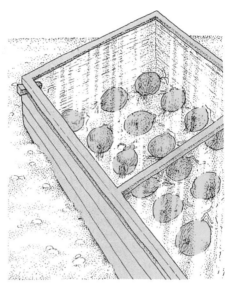

1 July to September. After lifting place the bulbs outside during dry sunny weather to dry and ripen further.

2 In wet weather arrange the bulbs in a single layer under a cloche or frame, or in a shed.

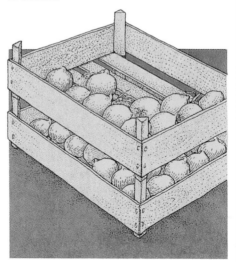

3 Turn the bulbs regularly to prevent diseases developing on the damp skins and wait 3-4 weeks for complete drying.

4 Store well-dried onions in trays with slatted bases and raised corners for good air circulation and easy inspection.

Shallots/Garlic

Shallots have a milder flavour than bulb onions and are sometimes grown in preference to onions in smaller gardens, because they keep better and are more easily grown. They are grown from small bulbs (offsets) saved from the previous year's crop. Each newly planted bulb produces a cluster of 8-12 daughter bulbs by the end of the season.

Cultivation
Soil and fertilizer requirements are the same as for spring-sown or planted bulb onions (see page 108). Early planting is very important for shallots, so dig the land as soon as it becomes available.

Planting Save sound, firm bulbs from the previous season, or buy sets. Small bulbs of about ⅓ oz weight (50 to the pound) are best to obtain maximum yield. Plant the bulbs in mid-February; space them 6 in apart in rows which are 8 in apart. Larger bulbs should be spaced 6 in apart with 12 in between the rows. Push the bulbs into the ground so that only the tips show above the soil surface. Alternatively, the bulbs can be planted in a shallow drill and then covered and firmed.

Birds or frost can lift the bulbs out of the soil and it is important to replant them immediately if this happens.

Weeds can be a problem, especially while the crop is young. Hoe carefully around the clusters, but do not damage the developing bulbs or they will not keep. Do not water unless the weather is very dry. Shallots suffer from the same pests and diseases as do onions (see page 110).

Shallots are ready for harvesting earlier than are spring-planted onions. They should be ready in July, and the bulbs will begin to ripen about three weeks before that. Draw away the soil from around the bulbs to encourage quicker ripening.

Harvesting
Dig up the clusters of bulbs when the leaves turn yellow. Separate them into individual bulbs and, in fine weather, leave them on the soil to dry off; dry them under protection in wet weather.

Remove soil and any loose, dry leaves from the ripened bulbs before storing them in nets in a cool, but frost-free place.

GARLIC

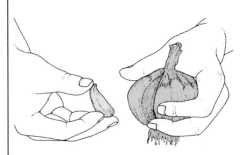

Garlic is a member of the onion family. Because of its strong flavour it is used sparingly in cooking. The plant is a perennial with long flat leaves and attractive white flowers. It can be grown in the open, in a pot or window-box, or in a cold greenhouse for early crops. The soil must be rich, moist and well drained.

Garlic grows best in a sunny position, because high temperatures are needed to ripen the bulbs. Before planting prepare the ground as for onion growing. Garlic seed is not readily available and so it is usually grown from bulb segments (cloves) saved from a previous crop or bought from a greengrocer. They are planted in February or March. Split a bulb into cloves. Plant them 1 in deep and 4 in apart with their pointed ends upwards. The rows should be 6-8 in apart. Do not press the cloves into the soil because this inhibits root development. Weed between the young bulbs with an onion hoe.

In late summer the stems and leaves begin to yellow and bend over. Loosen the bulbs gently out of the ground with a fork. Leave the bulbs on the soil surface to dry and ripen off in the sun. Do not handle the bulbs roughly because this may damage their necks and encourage rotting. Store well-dried bulbs of garlic in string bags in a cool but frost-free shed.

Shallots

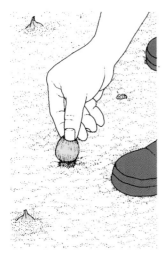

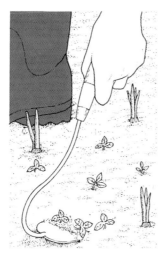

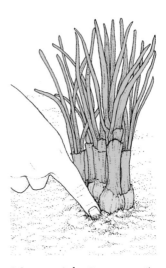

1 February. Push the bulbs into the ground so that their tops are just visible. Space them 6 in apart in rows 8 in apart.

2 March to June/July. Use a small onion hoe to keep the developing plants weed-free at all times. Remove any difficult weeds by hand.

3 June or July. Remove soil from around the clumps of onions by hand to speed up the ripening process.

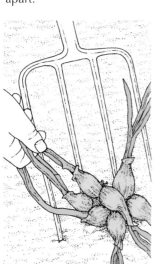

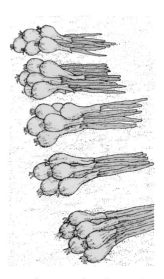

4 July onwards. Lift shallots when the leaves turn yellow. Remove soil from around the roots and rub off loose leaves.

5 At the same time, save small bulbs of about ⅓ oz in weight for next year's propagation material.

6 In fine weather, leave the bulbs in rows in the garden to dry out. In wet weather dry them under protection.

Leeks

Leeks are biennial plants grown as annuals. The stem-like collection of rolled leaves is eaten. Leeks have a long growing season and mature from September until May. They are winter-hardy and will tolerate very severe conditions. Leeks grow best in fertile, well drained soils of pH 6.5-7.5. Although they will tolerate slightly more acid or alkaline conditions, they do not thrive in heavy soils which remain wet in winter. Dig the soil well because they must be planted deeply or earthed up to produce the blanched appearance. The ground should be dug well during the winter before planting. Incorporate a 2-3 in layer of bulky organic manure or well-rotted garden compost. Do not give so much fertilizer that the plants become too lush and incapable of standing through frosty winter conditions. Apply 2-3 oz per square yard of a well-balanced compound fertilizer, such as a proprietary brand of Growmore, one or two weeks before planting.

Sowing and planting The germination and early growth of leeks are slow. The seeds need a soil temperature of at least 7°C/45°F to germinate. It is best to transplant leeks, using plants raised under cloches or in a heated greenhouse or purchased from a garden centre.

For early crops, sow in a seed tray in late January to early February in a greenhouse kept at 13°C/55°F. Prick out into other trays when the leaves have straightened up, spacing the seedlings 2 in apart each way. Maintain the temperature until hardening off the plants in a cold frame during March. Plant in late April.

Main crop leeks are sown outside in March to April for transplanting during late May or June. Sow the seed thinly in drills ½ in deep and in rows 6 in apart. June sowings, transplanted in July, produce crops the following spring. Plants can also be raised under cloches.

Planting Leek plants should be planted out when pencil-thick and 6-8 in high. Plant in rows 12 in apart. Make 2 in wide, 6 in deep holes with a dibber at 6 in intervals. After putting a seedling into the hole, do not replace the soil but fill each hole with water. This will settle sufficient soil around the roots.

Alternatively, leeks can be planted on the flat or in 2 in deep trenches and blanched by progressively drawing up soil around the plants during the growing season. Hoe off any weeds with an onion hoe. Water the plants only in very dry conditions, when 2 gal of water per 10 ft row should be applied weekly. Mulch crops grown on dry soils. On poor soils liquid fertilizer can be used, but do not apply fertilizer to leeks late in the summer because soft growth prone to frost damage will be produced. Leeks are relatively free from pests but susceptible to rust.

Harvesting
Early varieties are ready before Christmas but most leeks are harvested in mid-winter and spring. Lift them as required using a fork. Leeks are very hardy and they will remain usable until May.

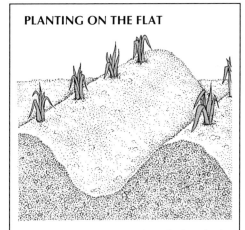

PLANTING ON THE FLAT

Blanched stems are produced when leeks are planted in holes, as described on the left, but longer white stems can be obtained if plants are earthed up. Plant the leeks 6 in apart in rows 12 in apart. Make holes 2-3 in deep and firm the soil around the base of each plant. Gradually draw up soil around the plants as they develop. Cardboard or paper collars may be tied around them to prevent soil getting into the plant centres.

Continue earthing up until November, when only the tops of the leaves should show above the soil.

Sowing

Planting

1 Late March to mid-April. Prepare a seedbed. Sow the seeds thinly in ½ in deep drills 6 in apart.

2 Early May. Thin the seedlings to ½-1 in apart. Firm the soil around the bases of the remaining seedlings.

3 Late May to early June. Make 6 in deep holes, with a dibber, every 6 in in rows 12 in apart. Drop 1 plant into each. Fill with water.

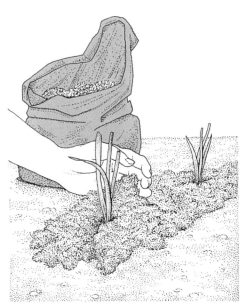

4 June until harvest. Mulch the crop once the seedlings are established. Water in dry spells.

5 November until April. Lift leeks as required with a fork. Trim off the roots and tips of the leaves. They are very hardy.

117

Carrots

Carrots are hardy biennial plants grown as annuals for their tasty roots. The long-rooted and intermediate varieties are mainly stored for use during the winter months, but successive sowings of short-rooted varieties produce bunching carrots in 10-12 weeks for use in summer salads from late spring to autumn. A 10 ft row of main crop carrots can yield 10-12 lb, depending on the variety.

Cultivation

Long-rooted varieties need a deep soil but short-rooted varieties are suitable for shallow soils and will grow in heavy conditions.

Soil and situation The ideal soil has a pH between 6.5 and 7.5, is well-drained, stone-free and of medium texture. It should not have been manured for at least a year before sowing. Thorough, deep winter digging is important. An application of balanced general fertilizer at 2-3 oz per square yard about a week before sowing will maintain fertility. Choose an open situation for carrots.

Watering If deprived of water carrots become woody and coarse. In dry weather apply water at a rate of 2 gal per square yard at weekly intervals. If the plants become too wet as a result of applications of water in rainy weather, the development of foliage as opposed to roots is encouraged.

Early carrots In February or March, sow short varieties under cloches or in frames in 1/2-3/4 in deep drills, 6 in apart. Always sow carrot seeds very thinly and thin the seedlings to 1 1/2-2 in intervals when they emerge. Young carrots mature from mid-May onwards for use in summer salads.

Alternatively, sow the seed outdoors every three or four weeks from March to August. These carrots are ready from June until November. Cover the later crops with cloches from September onwards.

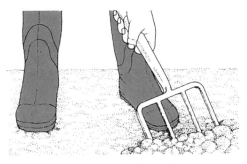

1 Winter. Dig the soil early so that a crumbly tilth develops. In spring apply fertilizer at 2-3 oz per square yard.

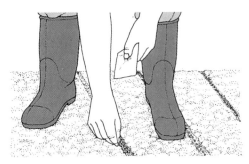

2 March onwards. Prepare a fine tilth. Sow the seed in 1/2-3/4 in deep drills 6 in apart. Cover the drills.

5 Throughout the summer. Pull early sowings by hand while they are young and tender.

6 October. Leave carrots in the ground where they have been grown but protect them from frost with a covering of straw.

Main crop carrots From April to June, sow intermediate or long varieties very thinly in ½-¾ in deep drills, with 6 in between the rows. These mature from August to October.

Hoe between the rows, and as soon as the first rough leaves appear, thin the seedlings until the distance between the plants is 2 in for short-, medium- and long-rooted varieties. Water the plants to re-firm them after thinning. The thinnings from larger varieties of carrots can be eaten.

Carrot flies are attracted by the smell of crushed foliage. The females lay eggs around the plants and the resulting larvae eat the roots. Attacks can be minimized by thinning the carrots late in the evening, removing the thinnings and watering afterwards. 'Sytan' and 'Fly Away' are relatively resistant.

Harvesting

Start pulling the early sowings by hand as soon as they are big enough to eat: Young tender roots are the sweetest. Gently ease up carrots for storage, with a fork, in October. Reject any that are unhealthy or damaged.

Remove the soil and foliage from carrots before storing them.

Storing Healthy carrots will last until March or April of the following year if they are stored properly in the right conditions. In particularly favourable districts they can be left in the ground and lifted as they are required. Protect them from severe frost with a covering of straw or similar material.

Pests and diseases

A reddish-brown discoloration of the foliage is often a symptom of carrot fly attack. Drench main crops in July or August with a pirimiphos-methyl-based insecticide. Apply pirimiphos-methyl or lindane dust at sowing time. Spray greenfly with derris or pirimicarb.

3 Thin the seedlings regularly after the first rough leaf appears to 2 in for short-, medium- and long-rooted varieties.

4 Water and firm the rows after thinning. Do not leave thinnings lying about. Hoe between the rows.

7 Alternatively, dig up carrots required for indoor storing with a fork. Select healthy roots only and twist off the foliage.

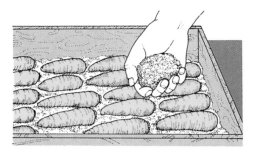

8 Pack the roots in boxes of dry sand, keeping individual roots apart, and store them in a cool frost-free place.

Parsnips

Parsnips are hardy biennial plants grown as annuals for the production of their edible roots. They have a long growing season and are among the first crops to be sown and the last to be harvested.

Cultivation

Parsnips need a well-drained soil of medium texture which must not have been manured for at least a year before sowing. Parsnips have a low nitrogen requirement, so take care not to over-manure and do not use nitrogen-rich fertilizers. Avoid stony soil. The best soil is slightly acid or neutral (pH 6.5-7.0) and the best position is open and sunny, although parsnips will tolerate a lightly shaded spot. Deep digging in the winter is essential because parsnips often root down to a depth of 2 ft. Dig the soil one spade deep and if the layer below is too packed for the feeding roots to penetrate easily, loosen it with a fork.

Such deep digging is not really necessary for short varieties, such as 'Avonresister', however. One to two weeks before sowing apply a balanced general fertilizer such as a brand of Growmore to the soil at 2 oz per square yard.

Sowing Sow parsnip seed in late February or early March, but avoid cold wet weather. A soil temperature of 7°C/45°F is needed. Always use fresh seed because older parsnip seed rapidly loses its ability to germinate. Even with fresh seed, the germination rate is low. Seedlings take up to four weeks to emerge in cold weather, though the normal period is seven to ten days. Take out 1/2-3/4 in deep drills. Keep a 12 in distance between rows for large-rooted varieties. If the soil is dry, water the drill before sowing. Sow the seeds in groups of three or four, with 6 in spacings between groups. Small-rooted varieties should be sown 3 in apart with 8 in between rows.

EXHIBITION PARSNIPS

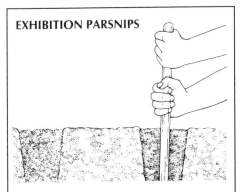

For long straight roots prepare the soil well and use a crowbar to make holes 3 ft deep and 6 in in diameter. Fill these conical holes with fine soil or potting compost and sow the seed in the usual way as early as possible. Throughout the growing season weed by hand and mulch with peat or black polythene to retain moisture.

Water regularly, especially when dry weather is forecast, to prevent any cracking of the long roots. Lift them as near as possible to the showing date. Remove the rootlets and cut off the tops. Protect exhibition parsnips from damage by wrapping them in damp cloth.

1 December. Dig the soil 1 spit deep. If the layer below is compacted break it up with a fork.

4 When the first true leaves appear thin the seedlings to leave the strongest plant at each station.

When the seedlings have their first true leaves carefully remove all but the strongest plant in each group. Weed between the seedlings by hand in the early stages. Carefully hoe between the plants later. If the shoulders of young plants are damaged, parsnip canker or other diseases may enter.

Never allow the soil to dry out. If the soil becomes dry and is then dampened by rain or watering, the parsnips often split. Water at a rate of 2 gal per square yard per week.

Harvesting
Lifting may begin when the foliage begins to die down, usually in late autumn or early winter. Use a fork to dig along the side of the row so as to lift the parsnips without breaking the roots.

Storing Leave parsnips in the ground throughout the winter and lift the roots as required. Frost is said to improve their flavour, although it is difficult to lift them in a severe winter. Parsnips can be stored in the same way as carrots (see page 119), but they tend to go soft. The remainder of the crop left in the ground can be lifted in March to make way for subsequent vegetables.

Pests and diseases
Young seedlings should be protected from carrot fly. Sprinkle pirimiphos-methyl or lindane along the seed row at sowing to protect the seedlings.

Parsnip canker develops in the crown of the plants and causes the roots to rot. There is no chemical control – prevention is the only answer – but the variety 'Avonresister' is resistant to the disease. Premature sowing, lime deficient soils and damage to roots by carrot fly larvae or careless hoeing are all likely to encourage the disease and weak or damaged roots are more vulnerable.

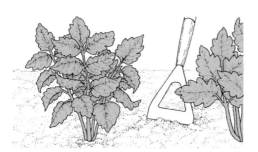

2 Late February. Apply fertilizer at 2 oz per square yard 1-2 weeks before sowing.

3 Late February-early March. Sow 3-4 seeds at 6 in intervals (3 in for small varieties) in ½-¾ in deep drills 12 in (8 in) apart.

5 Throughout the summer. Water frequently and hoe weeds regularly, taking care not to damage the shoulders of young plants.

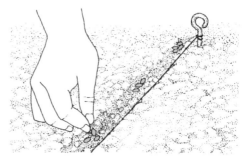

6 Late autumn onwards. When the foliage dies down lift parsnips as needed, using a fork to loosen the surrounding soil.

Turnips and swedes 1

Turnips and swedes are biennials grown mainly for their edible roots. Swedes are usually grown as a crop for winter harvesting, but turnips may be eaten all the year round. The young leaves or "turnip tops" are cut in March and April for use as a green vegetable and the roots may be eaten, either young or mature, for most of the year.

Cultivation

Turnips and swedes are brassicas and have broadly similar requirements to cabbages and Brussels sprouts.

Soil and situation They thrive in light, well-drained, firm soils of pH 6.0-7.0, rich in humus and water-retentive during the growing season. Main crop turnips and swedes require much the same methods of cultivation, although sowing dates and plant spacings differ. Soil preparation is identical and both crops are thinned in the seed rows to the appropriate distance and not transplanted.

The roots fork if they are grown in soil that has received dressings of fresh manure and so a site well manured for a previous crop should be used if possible. The site is dug over and prepared as a seedbed. Before sowing rake in a dressing of balanced general fertilizer at 3 oz per square yard to improve fertility. Then apply phoxim or diazinon and chlorpyrifos to control cabbage root fly from attacking the seedlings.

Watering The size and quality of both turnips and swedes are improved if ample water is available. If they are allowed to become dry at any stage the roots are likely to become woody and less palatable. Experimental work has shown that applications of 2 gal per square yard of water each week in dry weather increase both yield and quality, although flavour is slightly reduced.

Pests and diseases

Turnips and swedes, like other brassicas, are attacked by cabbage root fly and flea beetle; turnip gall weevil and aphids (with virus as a consequence) may also be troublesome. Swedes are less mildew-resistant than turnips.

EARLY BUNCHING TURNIPS

Bunched turnips are a good salad or early summer cooked vegetable. They must grow quickly with ample supplies of water. Dig the soil early in the autumn and cover the ground with cloches for 2-3 weeks before sowing the earliest crops which are protected. Prepare a fine seedbed and apply calomel dust against club-root and pirimiphos-methyl or lindane against cabbage root fly. Then sow short-leaved, early varieties from February onwards, at two week intervals for a succession. Mark out the ground in a 5 in crossed pattern with a stick, making the marks 1/2 in deep. Sow 2-3 seeds where the marks cross. Alternatively, sow the seed thinly in 1/2 in drills 12 in apart. Thin out the squared system to leave one plant per station. Row crops should be thinned to 4 in apart. Hoe very carefully in the early stages and never allow the soil to dry out.

Harvesting The roots are pulled like radishes. The first sowings mature during May when the roots are 2 in in diameter.

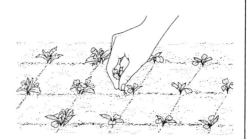

1 March. Thin grid-sown turnips to one plant per station. Thin row crops to 4 in apart at the same stage.

2 May. Pull the plants up by the leaves when the roots are 2 in in diameter.

Turnips

Turnips are fast-growing and are ready to eat 6-12 weeks after sowing. They germinate within a few days and must never become crowded in the rows. Thinning should take place as soon as possible when the first rough, true leaves appear (at about 1 in high) or the roots will not develop satisfactorily.

The main crop is sown in July or early August for winter use but earlier sowings from February (under cloches) onwards may be made, using early varieties. As these can be used in 6 or 8 weeks from sowing, when they are 1½-2 in in diameter, they are excellent for intercropping. Late sowings in September of winter types will also provide turnip tops as spring greens in March or April.

Swedes

Swedes have a sweeter taste than turnips and they are mainly grown for winter use, although immature swedes pulled in late summer make excellent eating. They should never be allowed to develop to the huge size of field-grown crops, which are often woody and more fitted for cattle than human consumption. They are slower to mature than turnips, taking 20-24 weeks from seed to develop fully, but are hardier and can be dug as required during the winter rather than stored. Cultivation is as for main crop turnips but swedes are sown from mid-May (cold areas) to mid-June in drills 15 in apart and they are finally thinned to 9 in apart in the rows.

PESTS AND DISEASES

Pests	Means of control
Aphids (and viruses)	
Cabbage root fly	see pages 31-33
Flea beetle	
Gall weevil	Lindane

Diseases	Means of control
Brown heart	Boron (applied as borax)
Club-root	*See* page 29

Main crop turnips

1 July. Rake into the prepared seedbed 3 oz of fertilizer per square yard.

2 Mid-July to early August. Water the seedbed the day before sowing. Draw out drills ½-¾ in deep and 12 in apart. If the soil is dry, dribble water into the drills and allow it to drain away.

Turnips and swedes 2

3 Then, sow the seed very thinly, cover, firm and gently rake over the soil. Apply calomel dust and a suitable insecticide to the seed row.

4 Late July or August. Thin the seedlings to 3 in apart as soon as they produce their first rough leaves when about 1 in high. Water them if the weather is dry.

7 Keep the rows free of weeds. In dry weather water at a rate of 2 gal per square yard each week.

8 Winter. Lift as needed in mild areas. In cold areas lift the roots carefully in late autumn when the leaves have turned yellow. Store them in boxes of sand, peat or dry soil in a frost-free shed.

5 Dust the seedlings with lindane or derris to combat flea beetle and turnip gall weevil.

6 August to September. Thin to 6 in apart as soon as the leaves of adjacent seedlings touch within the rows. Firm back the soil after thinning.

SWEDE SHOOTS AS GREENS

The roots of swedes lifted in mid-winter, if trimmed and packed closely in boxes of peat or soil and then placed in a garage or shed in semi-darkness, will sprout to produce nutritious, partly blanched growth that can be eaten like turnip tops.

TURNIP TOPS AS SPRING GREENS

In September sow the seed of winter varieties thinly in rows 3 in apart. Leave over winter without thinning. Cut the young leaves in March or April when they are 4-6 in high. If cut frequently they re-sprout several times.

Kohlrabi

Kohlrabi, like most brassicas, is grown as an annual although naturally it is a biennial. The swollen root-like stem is pleasantly and distinctively flavoured and it may be eaten raw, when it is useful for salads, or cooked like a turnip. It is in season from May until December. The green varieties are used for summer crops whereas the purple types are preferred for autumn and winter.

If grown well kohlrabi can be harvested eight weeks after sowing.

Cultivation

The general principles of brassica growing apply to kohlrabi (see page 50). A fertile well-drained soil of pH 6.0-7.0, rich in humus, is required. The plants must be given ample food and water and they must grow without check because otherwise the swollen stems become hard and woody. Soil requirements, seedbed preparation, and pest and disease control are the same as for turnips (see pages 122-3), but a top dressing of 1 oz per square

1 Early April to early September, at monthly intervals. Rake into the prepared seedbed 3 oz of fertilizer per square yard.

2 At the same time, water the seedbed. Draw out drills ½-¾ in deep and 12 in apart. On dry soil, dribble water into the drills and allow it to drain away.

5 May to late September. Thin again to 6 in apart when the leaves of adjacent seedlings touch within the rows. Firm the soil.

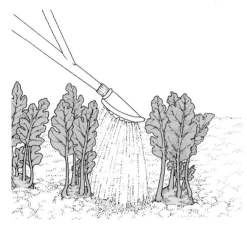

6 Water in a top dressing of 1 oz of nitro-chalk per square yard.

yard of nitro-chalk should also be applied if growth slows down.

Sowing For a succession of kohlrabi to harvest sow the seed in a prepared seedbed at monthly intervals from April to September. From April onwards use green varieties and from June until September use purple varieties. Make ½-¾ in deep drills, 12 in apart. Sow groups of three seeds at 6 in intervals and thin to one seedling per station. Alternatively, sow the seed thinly along the drills and thin at an early stage to 4-6 in apart.

Ample water (up to 2 gal per square yard each week) should be given to a kohlrabi crop in dry weather.

Harvesting

Pull the plants as needed from June onwards when the swollen stems are about the size of a tennis ball. If they are allowed to develop further than this they become woody and unpalatable.

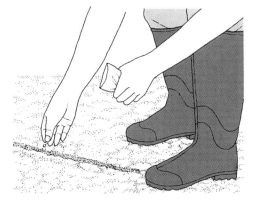

3 Sow 3 seeds at 6 in intervals. Alternatively sow and thin as for main crop turnips (see page 122). Apply calomel dust and a suitable insecticide.

4 Mid-April to mid-September. When the first rough leaves appear and the seedlings are 1 in high thin to 1 plant per station.

7 In dry weather, water at a rate of 2 gal per square yard each week. Keep the rows free of weeds.

8 June to December. Pull up the plants when the swollen stems are the size of a tennis ball.

Celeriac

Celeriac, also known as turnip-rooted celery, is a type of common celery in which the lower part of the stem and the main roots have become swollen. This swollen portion has the typical celery flavour and is an excellent substitute for it. Celeriac can be grated raw for use in salads and it is also useful as a winter vegetable for soups.

The plants are not earthed up and they achieve their full size during the autumn from March or April sowings.

Cultivation

Celeriac needs a long growing season and responds to good growing conditions. Good-sized celeriac requires a fertile soil which has had a heavy dressing of organic manure dug in during the winter. A base dressing of 2-4 oz per square yard of a balanced general fertilizer, such as a proprietary brand of Growmore, should be applied before planting.

Sowing Celeriac plants grow very slowly in the first two months from sowing. Sow the

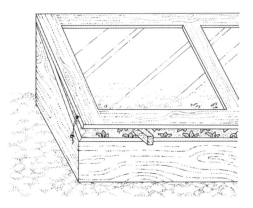

1 Late May. Harden off the seedlings by keeping them in a cold frame or under cloches for a few days.

2 Early June. Plant them at 12 in intervals in rows 15 in apart. Water in immediately after planting. Treat with a suitable insecticide to combat carrot fly.

4 During summer. Spray with dimethoate or malathion if celery fly attacks occur. Remove dead, decaying leaves and any side-shoots that appear.

5 July onwards. Give weekly applications of liquid manure in poor soils.

seed in mid-March under glass at a temperature of 18°C/65°F. The seedlings should be pricked out as soon as possible and transferred into small peat blocks, pots or seed trays at a spacing of 2-2½ in square. Keep the temperature at 13°-16°C/55°-60°F throughout propagation. Alternatively, the seed may be sown in a cold greenhouse or frame, or under cloches, in April.

Harden off the plants before planting out in late May. Plant them at 12 in intervals in rows

3 June to July. Top dress with nitro-chalk at 1 oz per square yard. Apply water at a rate of 4 gal per square yard each week in dry weather.

15 in apart. They require firm planting and should be watered in thoroughly. Treat the base of the plants with pirimiphos-methyl or lindane soon after transplanting as a precaution against carrot fly. Never allow them to go short of water during the growing period. Heavy waterings of up to 4 gal per square yard each week in dry weather will improve the size and quality of the crop. Top-dress with 1 oz per square yard of nitro-chalk in June or July. In poor soils weekly applications of liquid manure are beneficial. Keep the plants free of weeds. Remove old leaves as they die and break off any side-shoot growths which appear. This helps to produce a smoother swollen stem. If severe attacks of celery fly occur, spray with malathion.

Harvesting
The crops are ready from October onwards. In mild areas it is possible to leave celeriac in the ground until it is needed. Cover the plants with straw to prevent damage in very cold weather. Alternatively, they should be lifted carefully and trimmed of leaves and roots before storing in boxes of peat, sand or sawdust in a dry frost-free building.

Pests and diseases
Celeriac can suffer from the same pests and diseases as celery (see page 82).

6 October onwards. Lift, trim and store the crop in a frost-free building in boxes of dry peat or sand.

7 In mild areas leave celeriac in the ground until required but protect the crop against frost damage with a covering of straw or similar material.

Beetroot

Beetroots are biennial plants which are grown as annuals for their edible swollen roots. They usually have red flesh and the root shape may be round or long and tapering. Beetroots are good for intercropping as a useful catch crop; small beets mature in about 12 weeks.

Cultivation

Beetroot is in season from May or early June and throughout the winter.

Soil and situation Do not grow beetroot on freshly manured ground. Early crops can only be grown on well-drained, fertile soils, prepared in early spring, but autumn-maturing crops will tolerate heavier conditions. Beetroot grows best in soil with a pH of 6.5-7.5. A balanced fertilizer applied at 2-3 oz per square yard is sufficient to maintain growth. An open, shade-free site is preferable.

Sowing Beetroot "seeds" are actually fruits with two or three seeds contained within a cork-like pellet. They do not germinate well below 7°C/45°F, therefore warm spring weather is needed for early crops. To improve germination, soak the seeds for an hour or place them under running water before sowing.

Early crop In late February or early March, space-sow two or three seeds of round, bolt-resistant varieties at 4 in intervals under cloches or frames in rows 7 in apart. For outdoor sowing, the seeds are sown at the same spacing but from late March to early April. The plants are thinned to one per station.

Main crop beetroot

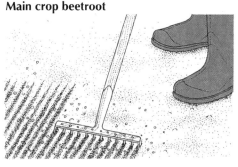

1 May or June. Apply a balanced general fertilizer to the prepared seedbed at 2-3 oz per square yard.

2 May or June. Soak the seeds of round or long varieties in water for an hour before sowing to improve germination.

5 Hoe very carefully around the developing plants with a short-handled hoe and water at 2 gal per square yard in dry weather.

6 August. Gently lift main crop beetroot with a fork when the roots are large enough to eat. Use immediately or store.

GLOBE
'Boltardy', 'Burpee's Golden',
'Detroit types', 'Moneta'
(monogerm).

LONG
'Cylindra', 'Forono'.

Main crop in May and June, space-sow two or three seeds of round or long varieties outdoors at 4-6 in intervals (depending on the type of beetroot) in rows 12 in apart.

Over-wintered beet In late June and July, sow two or three seeds of suitable round varieties at 3 in intervals in rows 12 in apart.

Watering In hot dry weather, water the plants at the rate of 2 gal per square yard each week, to maintain succulent, juicy growth. Give no more than this, however, because an excess of water may result in much leaf at the expense of root. Use black cotton to keep sparrows off the seedlings.

Hoe around the developing roots with a short-handled hoe. Damaged roots bleed readily so great care is needed.

Harvesting

Round varieties can be pulled as soon as they are large enough. Early sowings are ready from May to July. The main crop matures in August and should be lifted for use or stored.

Lift the young roots and twist or cut off the leaves. Store sound, disease-free roots in boxes of peat, sand or sawdust in a frost-free building. Distinct white concentric rings in the flesh when the roots are cut is a sign of old age. Inspect stored crops regularly and remove any old or diseased roots.

Round, late-sown beetroot is ready from October and in favourable locations this crop can be left in the ground during winter, if protected against frost with a covering of straw or similar material.

3 Space-sow 2-3 seeds at 4-6 in intervals (depending on variety) in 2 in deep rows, 12 in apart.

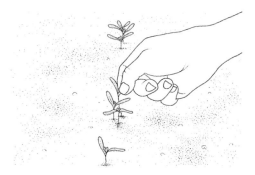

4 At the first true leaf stage thin to leave a single seedling at each station.

7 For storing, cut off the leaves to 1-2 in above each crown and remove dead or decaying leaves.

8 Arrange the beetroots in a box of sand. The roots should not touch. Keep the box in a cool frost-free place.

131

Radishes

Radishes are most commonly grown for salads but some varieties have much longer roots and these are cooked as a winter vegetable. Salad radishes have red, or red and white, skins and globular or cylindrical roots; winter radishes have white, black or pink skins.

Cultivation

Both radish crops grow quickly and they are often grown as a catch crop.

Soil and situation All radishes require a fairly rich and well-drained, but not freshly manured, soil to grow well. The soil must retain enough moisture to ensure rapid un-interrupted growth although too much moisture, or fertilizer, results in excessive leaf growth. You will then need to apply 1 oz per square yard of a balanced general fertilizer before each sowing.

An open situation is preferable for early and late sowings but sowings from June to August should be made in a slight shade between other crops.

Spring and summer radishes

The earliest salad radishes come from sowings made under cloches or frames in January and February. Successive outside sowings, without protection, can start in March and continue until August or September at two week intervals. Apply diazinon and chlorpyrifos or phoxim to the drills before sowing as a deterrent to root fly.

Sow the seed thinly in ½-¾ in deep drills which are 4-6 in apart. Alternatively, broadcast the seed on to the prepared seedbed and rake it in lightly. When the seedlings emerge,

thin, if necessary, until they are 1 in apart. Dust seedlings with derris, lindane or pirimiphos-methyl if flea beetles occur.

Keep the roots moist at all times. Dry, hot weather encourages hot-tasting radishes and during such periods apply water each week at the rate of 2 gal per square yard.

Winter radishes

Winter radishes are often 12 in long so a deep, friable soil is required. No fertilizer is needed when winter radishes are grown immediately after another crop, but on poor soils a general fertilizer should be raked in at a rate of 1 oz per square yard before sowing. Sow winter radishes in July or August.

Take out ½-¾ in deep drills 12 in apart, and control flea beetle as for spring crops. Sow the seed very thinly and when the seedlings are big enough to handle thin until

Spring radishes

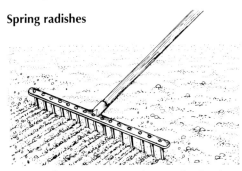

1 Late February. Prepare the seedbed, rake in 1 oz of a balanced general fertilizer per square yard and water well.

Winter radishes

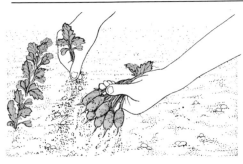

4 Six to eight weeks after sowing (3-4 weeks in midsummer). Pull the radishes as required when the roots are ¾ in diameter.

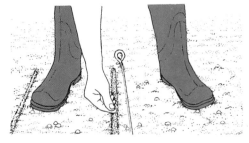

1 July or August. Space-sow the seed in groups of 3-4 at 6 in intervals in ¾ in deep drills, 12 in apart.

they are 6 in apart. Alternatively, the seed can be space-sown in groups of 3-4 at 6 in intervals and thinned to one per station.

The rapid growth of this crop means that it shades out weeds, except in the very early stages when careful hoeing is necessary. Regular watering in dry weather is important.

Harvesting

Pull spring and summer radishes when the roots are about 3/4 in diameter and they are firm and crunchy. Over-mature roots are hollow and unpalatable. The time taken to mature varies from 6-8 weeks at the end of the season to 3-4 weeks in midsummer.

Winter radishes are ready within 10-12 weeks of sowing. Lift them in late October, and store in boxes of dry sand for use as required. In mild areas leave them in the ground protected against frost.

EARLY SALAD RADISHES

The first sowing can be made in early January. Put cloches over the ground for 3-4 weeks beforehand to dry it out. Rake the soil into a fine tilth.

Using special short-topped varieties of radish broadcast the seed at 1/4 oz per square yard or sow it thinly in 1/2-3/4 in deep drills, 4-6 in apart. Water the seedbed thoroughly and keep the radishes moist throughout their life with regular applications of water.

Ventilate the crop on warm days because high temperatures under the cloche encourage leaf growth at the expense of roots.

Early salad radishes should be ready about eight weeks after sowing.

2 Early March. Draw out 1/2-3/4 in deep drills 4-6 in apart. Sow the seed thinly. Cover and firm.

3 After 10-14 days. Thin the seedlings to 1 in as soon as they can be handled easily. If the weather is dry water them each week.

2 After 7-10 days. Thin the seedlings to 1 plant per station as soon as they can be handled easily. Water after thinning.

3 Late October. Lift the roots carefully. Twist off the leaves and store them in dry sand in a cool frost-free place.

Salsify and scorzonera

Salsify and scorzonera are root crops widely grown in continental Europe, although less frequently cultivated in Britain. They are in season from October to April. Both produce long tapering roots that may reach 15 in or more in length.

Salsify roots are white-skinned and the flesh is said to have a fishy or oyster-like taste. The plant is commonly known as vegetable oyster. Scorzonera roots are black-skinned with white flesh which is not as strongly flavoured as salsify.

The young shoots or "chards" of both vegetables are also blanched and eaten as salad in the spring.

Cultivation
Both vegetables should be cultivated in the same way.

Soil A deep, well-drained soil of pH 6.0-7.5 is necessary. If possible, it should be free of stones so that the long roots can grow without obstruction. No fresh organic matter should be dug in before growing these crops because this causes the roots to fork. Dig the ground deply and rake in 2-3 oz per square yard of a balanced fertilizer, such as a brand of Growmore, before sowing.

Sowing Sow the seed in early April or May in drills ½ in deep and 12 in apart. Sow groups of two or three seeds at 6 in intervals along the drill. Thin to a single plant per station as soon as they are large enough to be handled.

Weeding Remove any weeds around each plant by hand. The roots are easily damaged and will "bleed" if a hoe is used carelessly. Salsify and scorzonera have thin, strap-like leaves that do not shade out weeds effectively, so it is important to remove all weeds regularly.

Watering Ample moisture must be available during the growing season to obtain the most succulent roots. A mulch helps to smother any weeds, conserves moisture and also reduces the risk of bolting during hot, dry weather.

Harvesting
Both salsify and scorzonera are hardy and the roots can be left in the ground to be lifted as required. When harvesting, lift very carefully because the long roots snap easily.

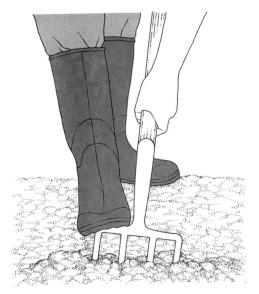

1 Early April. Dig the soil deeply and rake in 2-3 oz of a general balanced fertilizer per square yard.

4 Then, apply a 2-3 in layer of mulch. Water at the rate of 1 gal per square yard each week in dry weather.

2 Sow groups of 2-3 seeds at 6 in intervals in drills ½ in deep and 12 in apart.

3 May. Thin the seedlings to 1 plant per station when they are large enough to handle.

5 Autumn and winter. Leave the roots in the ground and use a fork to lift carefully as required. Avoid damaging the roots.

SALSIFY AND SCORZONERA SHOOTS

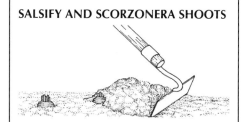

Salsify and scorzonera roots can be left in the ground to produce chards – edible top growth – the following spring. In autumn, cut off the old leaves, leaving about ½-1 in remaining above the soil. Earth up the roots to a depth of about 6 in so the shoots are blanched as they develop the following spring.

In March or April, scrape away the soil and cut the blanched shoots when they are 5-6 in long. Alternatively, allow the shoots to develop naturally, without earthing up, and cut them green when they are about 6 in tall. Green shoots are allegedly less palatable than blanched shoots.

Root artichokes

Both Jerusalem and Chinese artichokes are perennial vegetables grown for their edible stem-tubers. The Jerusalem artichoke is a member of the daisy family and closely related to the common sunflower. It grows to 10 ft in good conditions and produces knobbly, irregularly-round white or purplish tubers that can be boiled, fried or used in soups. It is a useful screen plant for hiding such features as compost heaps.

The Chinese artichoke, related to the deadnettle, is much shorter, reaching 1½-2ft. The white, elongated stem-tubers are pleasantly flavoured and they are used in the same ways as Jerusalem artichokes.

Cultivation
Both vegetables tolerate a wide range of soil conditions but they do not thrive in poorly drained or very acid soils. They grow well between pH 6.0-7.5 and crop reasonably even in relatively poor soils, although the tubers are then small and difficult to harvest. If possible grow them in fertile soil that has been well manured in the winter.

Planting Jerusalem and Chinese artichokes are propagated by tubers bought in or saved from the previous year's crop. Choose fairly large tubers and plant them during February or March. Jerusalem artichokes should be planted 6 in deep in rows 3 ft apart, with 12 in between each tuber in the rows. Chinese artichokes are planted to the same depth, and at the same time, but at 9 in intervals in rows that are 18 in apart.

Keep them well watered during dry spells since tuber development is reduced in dry soils. Jerusalem artichokes require supporting unless they are grown in a very sheltered site; Chinese artichokes have a bushy habit and do not require supports.

Earth up Jerusalem artichokes – rather like potatoes – in early summer to reduce wind rocking and encourage tuber formation close to the surface.

In poor soils from June to August apply feeds of liquid manure at 2-3 week intervals to improve tuber size.

Jerusalem artichokes

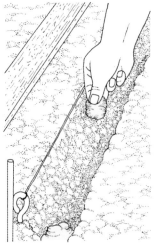

1 February or March. Plant tubers about the size of a small egg at 12 in intervals in 6 in deep holes in rows 3 ft apart.

2 May or June. Tie the plants to wires 9-12 in apart, stretched between stakes about 2 ft apart.

3 At the same time, earth up Jerusalem artichokes to protect them against windrock and encourage tuber formation near the surface.

Harvesting

Cut down the plants when frost has killed the foliage to leave about 6 in of stem above ground. Jerusalem artichokes can be left in the ground until required but Chinese artichokes are slightly less hardy. Unfortunately the tubers of both plants go soft and dry out when they are lifted. It is usually better to leave them in the ground and protect them with a covering of straw, or similar material, if severe weather is likely.

Always keep enough good-sized tubers for next year's crop but take great care to remove all tubers from the ground. Even the smallest tubers will grow again if they are left behind. The resulting plants can then be a nuisance among other crops.

Pests and diseases

Soil pests such as slugs and wireworms may cause some damage to Jerusalem and Chinese artichokes. For controls see page 33. Otherwise both crops are relatively free of problems.

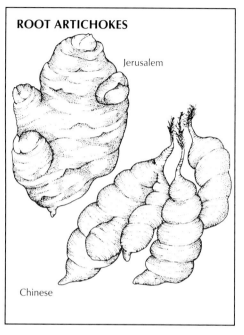

ROOT ARTICHOKES

Jerusalem

Chinese

Chinese artichokes

4 June to August. Water the plants regularly in dry weather at 2 gal per square yard. In poor soils apply liquid fertilizer every 2-3 weeks to improve size.

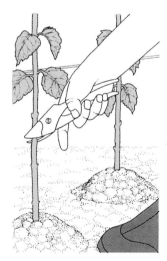

5 Autumn. Cut top growth down leaving 6 in of stem above ground. Leave the tubers in the ground, for lifting as needed, but protect against frost.

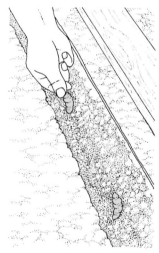

February or March. Plant the tubers at 9 in intervals in 6 in deep holes in rows that are 18 in apart.

Potatoes 1

The potato is the most widely grown vegetable in temperate zones. It is a South American perennial but it is only half-hardy in Europe. Late frost in May kills the emerged leaves of a potato crop, and the first autumn frosts kill the remaining foliage.

The potato is grown for its edible tubers and it is propagated from specially grown tubers ("seed") saved from the previous season. It is possible to save tubers from home-grown crops, but this is not advisable because potato plants and tubers soon become infected by debilitating virus diseases and if infected, crop yield and quality suffer. Virus-free "seed" is produced in areas where aphids that spread viruses are less of a problem. Certified seed potatoes should always be used.

Always use small "seed" tubers because large seed potatoes produce too many sprouts. For the maximum yield and to prevent crowded tubers being forced to the surface and "greening", small seed tubers producing only two or three sprouts are ideal for propagating purposes.

Potatoes are classified according to the time at which they mature. Earlies are ready to eat in June or July; second earlies in August and early September; and main crops mature in September and October.

Tuber skin colour also varies but white or red-skinned varieties are most common; the flesh of potatoes is usually white but occasionally pale yellow.

Cultivation

Soil and situation Potatoes tolerate a wide range of soils but they grow best in deep, fertile, well-drained soils with sufficient bulky organic manure to retain moisture in dry weather. Do not apply lime before planting potatoes because they grow best at a pH of 5.0-6.0 and alkaline conditons favour potato scab disease. Dig in a dressing of 15-20 lb per square yard of well-rotted compost or manure in the autumn.

In spring, fork over the ground and rake in a general fertilizer, such as a proprietary brand of Growmore, at the rate of 4 oz per square yard. A deep tilth is needed for earthing-up. Plant potatoes in an open site but not in a frost pocket.

1 Spring. Fork over the ground and rake in general balanced fertilizer at 4 oz per square yard.

2 March to April. Take out 6 in deep drills, 24 in apart for earlies, 27-30 in apart for later crops (according to the variety being grown).

FIRST EARLIES
'Maris Bard', 'Swift', 'Winston'.

SECOND EARLIES
'Kestrel', 'Maris Peer', 'Nadine'.

MAIN CROP
'Cara', 'Desiree', 'Maris Piper'.

SALAD TYPES
'Charlotte', 'Nicola', 'Pink Fir
Apple', 'Roseval'.

Plant potatoes in an open site but not in a frost pocket.

Planting Seed potatoes should be about 1 oz in weight, the size of a small hen's egg. Plant the tubers with the "rose" end upwards in 6 in deep drills, with 12 in between early potato tubers and 16 in between second earlies and main crops. Cover the planted drills immediately after planting. Draw up the soil to produce a mould 4-6 in high over each row.

Early potatoes Plant at the end of March in rows 24 in apart with 12 in between tubers.

Potatoes are usually grown in ridges which are formed gradually during the season by earthing-up (ridging) every two to three weeks. Cultivate and hoe between the initial mounds to provide sufficient loose soil for earthing. Use a draw hoe to pull up soil into ridges around growing plants.

Watering Earlies should be watered at the rate of 3-4 gal per square yard every 10-14 days to increase yield from an early stage of growth. If they are watered at the "marble"

stage (when the small developing tubers are the size of a marble, approximately $\frac{1}{2}$ in diameter) and not before, at the rate of 3-4 gal per square yard, they mature earlier.

Main crops should be given 4 gal per square yard at flowering time, which markedly increases yield and depresses scab.

Harvesting
Early potatoes should be ready about three months after planting, in June and July. The potatoes should be ready when the flowers are fully open. Lift as needed.

Second early and main crop potatoes should be lifted from August onwards.

Use a flat-tined fork to avoid too much damage to the tubers when lifting potatoes. Leave the tubers on the soil surface for two to three hours to dry. In wet conditions dry the tubers in a garage, a cold frame or under cloches. Make sure that all the potatoes are lifted so that no disease is carried over to the next year by overlooked tubers.

Storing Store only sound, healthy tubers. Any damaged potatoes should be used or discarded immediately. Store in a frost-free

3 At the same time, place the seed tubers in the drills at 12 in intervals for earlies, 16 in for second early and main crops, with the buds or "eyes" upwards.

4 Use a draw hoe to cover the drills. Draw up soil from both sides to produce 4-6 in high mounds over the planted rows.

Potatoes 2

building. Boxes with raised corner posts are ideal because it is easy to inspect the tubers. Keep them in the dark or cover with black polythene, to prevent the tubers turning green. Large quantities of potatoes can be stored in outside clamps. After lifting leave them to dry out for several hours, having removed the stems. Heap them up underneath straw and leave them to "sweat" for a couple of days before mounding up with earth to form a clamp.

Pests and diseases

Use virus-free seed to avoid the problems of potato virus diseases. Slugs, wireworm, cutworm and potato cyst eelworm and their control are described on pages 32-33. Common scab (see page 29) is rarely a serious problem, although it is worse on alkaline soils. Ample watering is a good deterrent.

5 During the summer, hoe regularly in the furrows between the ridges. Water during dry weather.

Potato blight This is the worst fungal disease of the crop and it can be particularly bad in warm, humid conditions from July onwards. The symptoms appear first on the leaves as yellow blotches on the upper surface. A white fungal growth may be seen underneath the leaves. The blotches turn brown and whole leaves are killed in severe attacks. Fungal spores are washed into the soil, where they can also infect the developing tubers. Very regular spraying is the major method of control. Spray the plants with bordeaux mixture or mancozeb at ten day intervals when conditions favour the disease.

8 June to July. Lift early potatoes when the flowers are fully open, using a flat-tined fork to avoid excessive damage to tubers.

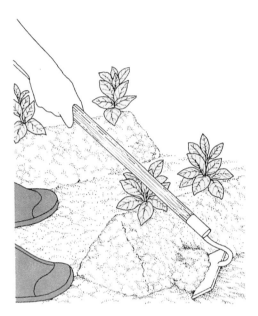

6 Hoe the soil from the furrows into ridges around the growing plants at 2-3 week intervals, until the ridges are 12-15 in high.

7 July onwards. At 10 day intervals, in warm humid conditions, spray all the surfaces of the leaves with an appropriate fungicide for potato blight control.

9 August onwards. Lift second early and main crop potatoes when the tops have died down.

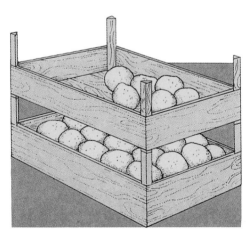

10 Store in a frost-free building in boxes with raised corner posts for easy inspection.

Potatoes 3

CHITTING POTATOES

Place a single layer of tubers – "rose" end upwards – in boxes or trays and keep them in a light, airy place such as a cool greenhouse. Begin the process in early February so that sturdy shoots about 3/4-1 in long will have formed prior to planting in late March. Chitted tubers grow away quickly when planted and are particularly useful for early crops which have a relatively short growing period. It may be worth while chitting second early or main crop varieties in areas where late planting is necessary.

Potatoes are normally grown outdoors as described on the previous pages. There are alternative systems, however, for growing out-of-season potatoes or for less labour-intensive cultivation of this basic vegetable crop.

Out-of-season potatoes

Very early potatoes can be grown in a greenhouse to mature in March or April. Plant chitted seed in a slightly heated greenhouse at a temperature of 7°-10°C/45°-50°F in January and grow in the same way as outdoor crops. Never allow the temperature to get very high or too much foliage will be produced and few tubers. Keep the plants moist.

Growing in pots

Plant 2 or 3 chitted tubers in large pots which are at least 12 in wide and deep, containing good garden soil.

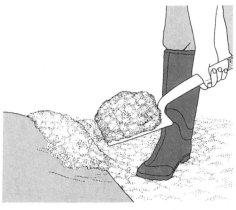

3 Cover the ridges with a 36 in wide length of black polythene and bury the edges to leave a 24 in wide strip exposed.

4 Make slits with a sharp knife above each tuber where the shoots have pushed against the polythene.

An alternative is to grow the plants in pots. Plant 2-3 chitted tubers in a large box or pot containing good garden soil. Keep the pots in a slightly heated greenhouse and grow as for the greenhouse crop.

Early outdoor plantings can be covered with glass cloches or polythene tunnels to speed development and give protection against frost. Cover the cloches with sacking when frosts are forecast.

Non-cultivation system

Potatoes can be grown without earthing up. Water the ground well before planting. In April, push chitted tubers into the soil and cover and mound over the drills. Cover with a black polythene sheet to prevent greening and weed growth, to warm the soil and to conserve moisture. Make a slit above each tuber. Bury the edges of the polythene by pushing them into the soil with a spade.

Slugs and wireworms thrive in the conditions provided by polythene. Control slugs by scattering methiocarb or metaldehyde slug pellets around the mounds.

When the shoots emerge they begin to push up through the slits in the sheet towards the light. Roll back the sheet to expose the tubers for harvesting or take them out as required through the slits.

Growing under black polythene

1 April. Water the ground and push chitted tubers into the soil at the same spacings as for outdoor potatoes.

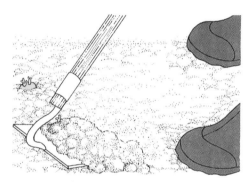

2 Cover and mound over the drills. Scatter slug pellets around the slightly mounded ridges.

5 May. As the shoots emerge they push up through the slits in the polythene.

6 July. As the tubers develop, roll back the polythene sheeting to expose the potatoes for harvesting.

Tomatoes 1

In Britain tomatoes are usually grown in greenhouses, but they can be grown outside in mild, sheltered locations, and the protection of frames or cloches makes it possible to grow them in less favourable areas. There are many varieties of tomatoes, most of which are long-stemmed and crop over a long period. Bush varieties are less common but, because they are short jointed, they do not require staking and trimming. Tomato fruits are usually red, although some yellow-fruited varieties are available.

Raising tomato plants

Tomatoes are transplanted into their final positions, and the same procedure is used for raising seedlings for both greenhouse and outdoor crops. Alternatively, it may be more convenient to purchase the plants from a reliable nursery or garden centre.

GROWING SYSTEMS

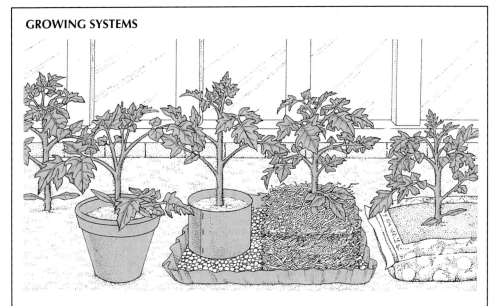

Tomatoes may be grown directly in the greenhouse soil but, after a number of years, pests and diseases may build up. These are best controlled by soil sterilization, no easy task in home gardens.

An alternative is to grow the plants in large 9 in pots filled with a proprietary or home-made compost and stand them on the greenhouse soil. The roots eventually come out of the pot bottom, but most of them will be in clean compost.

Ring culture is very similar, except that the pots are placed on a 3-4 in deep bed of pebbles or ashes which is isolated from the soil by a layer of polythene.

It is also possible to grow tomatoes directly into straw bales which stand on a polythene sheet on the greenhouse soil. The bales must come from fields that have not been sprayed with hormone weed-killers, however. Sprinkle 2-3 oz of a nitrogenous fertilizer, such as nitro-chalk, on to the surface of each bale and water it in thoroughly. Allow 2-3 weeks for straw decomposition and fermentation to begin before planting in a small bed of compost on top of the bales.

Growing bags contain peat and permit complete isolation from the greenhouse soil. They are also useful for roof gardens, patios, balconies and outside against sunny walls. Growing bags contain few nutrients, and so correct watering and feeding is critical.

GREENHOUSE
'Alicante', 'Dombito' (beefsteak), 'Shirley'.

OUTDOOR (CORDON)
'Gemini', 'Moneymaker', 'Super Marmande'.

OUTDOOR (BUSH)
'Roma', 'Tornado', 'Tumbler'.

CHERRY TYPES
'Gardener's Delight', 'Mirabelle' (yellow), 'Sweet 100'.

STRIPED
'Tigerella'.

Seed sowing

In a heated greenhouse kept at 18°C/65°F it is possible to raise plants for planting in about eight weeks. Outdoor planting does not take place until early June, but cold glass tomatoes can be planted in mid- to late April. Heated greenhouse crops can be planted from mid-February onwards. Sow the seed about eight weeks before the anticipated planting date. Sow thinly into seed trays or pans. Cover lightly with sieved compost and maintain the temperature at 18°C/65°F (see page 158). Germination and emergence occurs in 7-10 days. Do not sow too thickly or damping-off diseases quickly spread. Keep the seedlings evenly moist without water-logging them.

Pricking out

Carefully remove the seedlings from the tray

Plant raising

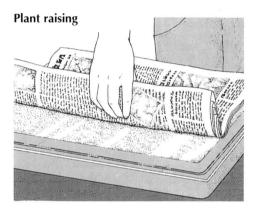

1 Sow the seed thinly in trays 8 weeks before planting. Cover with ⅛ in of sieved compost and water before covering with glass and newspaper. Keep at 18°C/65°F. Turn the glass daily.

2 Ten to twelve days after sowing, gently remove the seedlings by inserting a small dibber beneath the roots. Fill 3 in peat pots with potting compost, making holes big enough to take the seedlings.

3 Plant each seedling at the same depth as in the tray. Water to firm, then water little and often. Reduce the temperature to 16°C/60°F when the plants begin to shade each other. Liquid feed before planting.

4 Plant tomatoes when they are 6-9 in tall with the flowers on the first truss just opening. Water well before and after planting.

Tomatoes 2

or pan at the true leaf stage. Hold them very gently by the leaves and prick them out singly into individual pots, such as 3 in peat or plastic pots, which contain a proprietary potting compost. Water them gently to firm the compost around the roots. Keep the young plants in the greenhouse at the same temperature (18°C/65°F).

Good light conditions are essential for growing sturdy, healthy tomato plants; shaded, overcrowded conditions must be avoided. Water the plants sparingly – little and often is better than fluctuations between drought and waterlogging – and liquid feed with a balanced nutrient solution as the time for planting approaches. Reduce the temperature to 16°C/60°F when the plants begin to shade each other. It may necessary to support each plant with a small, split cane if it becomes too tall.

The planting stage

The ideal time for planting is when the flowers on the first truss are opening. The plants should then be 6-9 in tall. Destroy any plants affected by virus diseases.

Tomatoes in the greenhouse

Greenhouse tomatoes are generally liquid fed and it is unusual to use solid fertilizers for them. If plants are grown in the soil then it is important to double dig and incorporate well-rotted organic manure or compost with the lower spit. Water the plants thoroughly before planting and use a trowel to make holes which accommodate the roots without crowding. Plant with the top of each root ball level with the soil surface. Plants raised in peat pots should be planted complete with the pot. Make sure that the peat pot is very wet and, if drying out is likely, tear down one side of the pot wall before planting. Then water in thoroughly and keep the plants moist until the roots are established.

Supporting Whatever the support system, space the plants about 18 in apart each way. Greenhouse tomatoes are usually supported by strings suspended from overhead wires. Attach a length of soft garden string loosely around the stem beneath the lowest true leaf. Tie the other end to a wire attached to the greenhouse and stretched above the row of tomato plants. Twist each tomato plant

Greenhouse tomatoes

Supporting

1 Mid-February onwards. Make holes with a trowel and plant tomato plants 18 in apart each way with the top of each root ball level with the soil surface. Water thoroughly.

2 At the same time attach soft string loosely around the stem beneath the lowest true leaf of each plant. Tie the other end of the string to a wire stretched above the row.

3 Snap or cut off side-shoots and basal shoots. Shaking the plants in this way or spraying with a fine droplet spray improves fruit setting by dispersing pollen. Water and feed.

loosely around the string as it grows upwards. Do not make the string too tight or the tomato stem will be constricted and damaged. Alternatively, the plants can be supported by tying them loosely with soft string to bamboo canes.

Trimming and de-leafing Side-shoots develop in the axils (angles between the leaves and stems) of each leaf and must be removed while they are still small. Otherwise they use up water and nutrients intended for the main plant. Snap off the small side-shoots between thumb and forefinger. This is best done early in the morning when the plants are turgid and the shoots snap off easily. Avoid pulling out side-shoots, because irregular and untidy wounds produce scars into which fungal diseases easily spread. If side-shoots become too large it is best to cut them out carefully with a sharp knife. When the plants are 4-5 ft tall it usually helps to remove the lower leaves up to the first truss. This allows more light into the bottom of the plant and improves the air circulation and, hence, reduces the chance of fungal diseases. Always cut off the leaves cleanly with a sharp knife.

Watering and feeding Watering and feeding of greenhouse tomatoes is critical and requires a great deal of attention. Soil-grown plants are the easiest to manage because the soil acts as a buffer and a reservoir for nutrients and water. Completely isolated systems, such as growing bags, are more difficult because they contain few inherent nutrients and the small volume of peat can only hold a small amount of water. Overwatering growing bags is dangerous and quickly kills off plant roots, causing wilting of the plants. Little and often watering is time-consuming and a nuisance, but it is the only satisfactory method with growing bags which may need watering three or four times during a hot summer day. Mix a well-balanced liquid feed with the water. It is best to follow the instructions, although it is as well to understand that nitrogen encourages vegetative growth of the plant whereas potassium improves fruit quality.

Pollination and fruit setting There is usually no difficulty in getting tomato flowers to set fruit. Occasionally, however, problems occur and fruit setting is improved by vibrating the

4 When the plants are 4-5 ft tall cut off the lower leaves (up to the first truss) on each plant. Remove yellowing, decaying or diseased leaves on sight.

5 When 6 or 7 trusses have set fruit, or when the plants may be reaching the greenhouse roof, remove the growing points 2 leaves beyond the top truss.

6 Harvest tomatoes in the greenhouse as needed. Pick each fruit with the calyx still attached.

Tomatoes 3

bamboo cane or string, by tapping the flower trusses, or by spraying the plants over with water to disperse pollen.

Stopping Cold greenhouse tomato plants are unlikely to produce more than six or seven trusses in a normal season. It is best, therefore, to remove the growing point of each plant when it reaches the roof of the greenhouse, or two leaves beyond the top (sixth) truss.

Harvesting

Pick the fruits as required. Ripening takes place rapidly once the tomatoes begin to turn orange.

Pests and diseases

Glasshouse whitefly is the most common pest of protected tomatoes. Pyrethrum, bifenthrin or permethrin sprays may control the pest, but biological control with the wasp *Encarsia formosa* is preferable.

Fungal diseases such as grey mould (*Botrytis cinerea*) and leaf-mould are particularly troublesome in humid, poorly ventilated conditions. Botrytis is also encouraged when plants are soft or have trimming and side-shooting scars. Remove any yellowing, damaged or decayed leaves immediately.

The foliage of outdoor tomatoes can be attacked by potato blight and must be sprayed with a fungicide in July (see page 141).

Soil-borne pests, such as eelworms, produce yellow and stunted growth and virus diseases, such as tobacco mosaic virus (T.M.V.), cause mottling of the leaves, reduced plant vigour and poor fruit set. Eelworms can be avoided by not using the greenhouse soil, and T.M.V. resistant varieties are the only way of avoiding the virus.

The most common nutrient deficiency is caused by a lack of magnesium. The condition develops from the bottom of the plant upwards and produces a marked yellowing between the leaf veins. Magnesium deficiency can often be corrected by sprinkling a pinch of Epsom salts (magnesium sulphate) around each plant and watering it in.

Outdoor tomatoes

Outdoor tomatoes may be planted from early June onwards in mild temperate locations such as southern England. Frames and cloches can be used to protect young plants and they can also be used to ripen fruit at the end of the season.

Cultivation

Choose a well-sheltered site such as a south-facing wall. Tomatoes do not tolerate cold, windy conditions and it may be necessary to use polythene or netting windbreaks. It is also important that the soil allows rapid, uninterrupted growth. Dig in well-rotted organic manure at 15 lb per square yard in the winter. Incorporate 3-4 oz per square yard of a general, balanced tomato fertilizer before planting in early June. Later in the season it may be necessary to feed the plants with a proprietary tomato liquid feed.

Planting The technique is the same as for greenhouse plants but outdoor tomatoes are usually grown directly in the soil. Alternatively, pots or growing bags can be placed on the soil or on balconies or patios. Soil-grown plants should be spaced 18 in apart in each direction. Warm the soil with cloches for 2-3 weeks before planting or spread black polythene over the soil surface and cut holes through which to plant the tomatoes. The polythene conserves moisture and sup-

Supporting and training When tomatoes are grown outside they are usually tied to 5 ft bamboo canes but there are proprietary plastic-covered wire supports for use in conjuction with growing bags. Tie the stems to the canes with soft garden string at 12 in intervals. Bush tomatoes are stocky in growth and no supporting or trimming is necessary for them. Side-shoots must be removed from other varieties, however.

Stopping It is unlikely that more than four trusses will ripen outside. Stop the plants when four trusses have set by pinching out their growing points two leaves beyond the fourth truss. Spray against potato blight.

Weed control Weeds can be removed by hand weeding or careful hoeing.

Harvesting

Fruits can be ripened on the plant by laying the stems along the ground on a bed of straw and then covering them with cloches.

Outdoor tomatoes

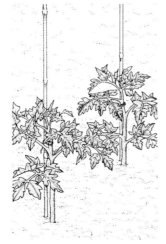

Training

1 Early June. Before planting apply 3-4 oz per square yard of tomato fertilizer to the soil. Plant 18 in apart each way and water well.

2 Immediately after planting, loosely tie the stems with soft garden string to bamboo supports at 12 in intervals.

3 Remove any side-shoots that develop on tomato plants (except bush varieties).

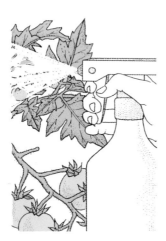

4 Stop each long-stemmed plant 2 leaves beyond the fourth truss as soon as the fruits being to swell.

5 Continue to remove any side-shoots induced to grow as a result of stopping. Spray against potato blight. Water and liquid feed regularly.

6 Mid-September. Cut the strings and lay the plants on a bed of straw. Cover with cloches and continue to water without wetting the fruit.

Cucumbers 1

Cucumbers are sub-tropical plants grown for their green-skinned fruits which are used raw in salads. Greenhouse cucumbers are long-stemmed types and produce long, cylindrical fruits, whereas outdoor ridge types are trailing or bushy and usually have shorter, stumpy fruits.

Greenhouse cucumbers

Greenhouse cucumber plants are raised in a heated house with a temperature of 21°-25°C/70°-75°F. It takes about 4-5 weeks from sowing until planting can take place at the end of March. Do not plant in unheated greenhouses until the end of May.

Sowing Cucumber seed has somewhat erratic germination and should be "chitted" before sowing. Place the seeds on moist kitchen towelling in a closed plastic container and keep in a warm place such as an airing cupboard. Germination begins in 2-3 days and the germinating seeds can then be sown into their individual containers. Put single seeds into 3 in peat or plastic pots filled with a proprietary potting compost such as John

Innes No. 1. Maintain the temperature at 21°C/70°F. Keep the developing plants well watered and support and tie them to small split canes. Keep the greenhouse atmosphere as humid as possible and liquid feed the plants with a proprietary, balanced general fertilizer to maintain good growth.

Growing systems

Greenhouse cucumbers can be planted directly into the soil but it is better to use growing-bags, pots or straw bales. Straw bales should not have been sprayed with hormone weedkillers and must be treated and fermented before planting. Make a small compost bed, using John Innes No. 3, along the middle of each bale and plant the cucumber into the compost. Growing bags can also be used for greenhouse cucumbers. Allow two plants per bag. Alternatively, grow each plant in a 9-10 in pot filled with a potting compost such as John Innes No. 3.

Growing

Greenhouse cucumbers grow best at high

Chitting

Sowing

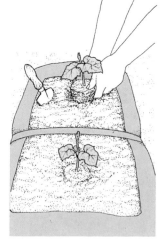

1 Late February. Sprinkle cucumber seeds on moistened kitchen tissue in a plastic container. Cover and keep in a warm place (21°C/70°F), such as an airing cupboard.

2 Two or three days later, sow each chitted seed ³/₄ in deep in 3 in pots of potting compost. Keep at 21°C/70°F. Water and feed, and support with split canes if necessary.

3 Late March (late May in unheated greenhouses). Plant 2 plants into a standard-sized growing bag. Give small amounts of water and liquid feed regularly.

GREENHOUSE
'Brunex', 'Pipinex'.

OUTDOOR
'Burpless Tasty Green', 'Crystal Apple' (round fruited), 'Jazzer', 'Venlo Pickling' (gherkin).

temperatures and high humidities. They grow rapidly and need constant watering and liquid feeding, although the compost must never become waterlogged. Plants must be supported and trimmed by twisting them around strings or by tying to bamboo canes (see page 148). Pinch out the growing points when the plants reach the roof.

The older greenhouse cucumber varieties have both male and female flowers, but modern introductions have female flowers only. Greenhouse cucumbers are produced without pollination and it is important that any male flowers are removed because the fertilization of female flowers results in bitter-tasting cucumbers. There is a small "embryo" cucumber behind each female flower.

Pinching and trimming

Pinching and trimming are also important. The first cucumbers produced form in leaf axils directly on the main stem. When they have developed, lateral shoots should be allowed to come out from the leaf axils and these, too, produce cucumbers. Stop the laterals after two leaves. More cucumbers will then develop in the axils of the lateral leaves. Use a sharp knife to trim cucumbers and handle them carefully because they snap easily.

Harvesting

From May onwards cut the cucumbers with a sharp knife as they reach the required size. The plants will regulate the number of fruits which they produce and the excess will drop off at a young stage. Do not be tempted to keep too many cucumbers per plant since individual fruit size will be reduced.

Pests and diseases

Glasshouse red spider mite and glasshouse whitefly are likely to be most prevalent. Pirimiphos-methyl may be used to control them. Biological control with the wasp *Encarsia formosa* can be used against whitefly, and the predatory mite *Phytoseiulus persimilis* against red spider. Powdery mildew is the most common disease. It covers the leaves with a white powdery growth and it is controlled with carbendazim.

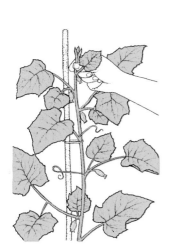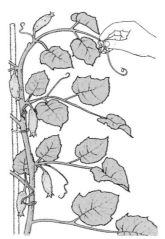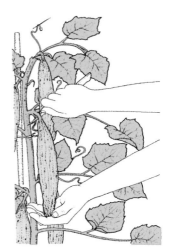

4 April. Support the plants by tying them to bamboo canes and pinch out the growing points when the main stems reach the greenhouse roof.

5 April onwards. Allow the cucumbers to develop sequentially up the main stems. Keep single laterals in each leaf axil and stop them at 2 leaves. Remove male flowers.

6 May onwards. Cut cucumbers with a sharp knife when they reach the required size.

Cucumbers 2

Outdoor cucumbers

Ridge cucumbers and gherkins can be grown outside in cool temperate climates, but earlier crops are obtained if plants are covered with cloches in the early stages. Pollination is necessary for the production of outdoor cucumbers and gherkins so both male and female flowers must be retained. The Japanese climbing outdoor varieties available today produce smoother, longer cucumbers but they require training on netting or wire to a possible height of 6 ft.

Soil A moisture-retentive and fertile soil is essential. Prepare planting or sowing positions by making holes and filling them with a good fork load of well-rotted organic manure or compost. Cover with soil to make a mound.

Allow 36 in between ridge cucumbers and 24 in between gherkins. It is possible to incorporate 1 oz of general purpose fertilizer around each mound but regular liquid feeding of developing plants with a proprietary product is generally more convenient.

Sowing Plants can be raised in the same way as greenhouse cucumbers and then transplanted. This is difficult and laborious, however, and the outdoor types are readily checked by transplanting. Consequently it is better to sow the seed directly outside. Pregerminate the seeds to ensure 100 per cent success or sow three seeds at each station where a plant is required.

Sow outdoor cucumbers in early May in mild locations such as southern Britain but not until early June in less favourable areas. Push the seeds ¾ in deep into the soil and thin to one per station later if necessary. Germination is quicker if the soil is covered with small individual cloches or jars.

Growing

Ridge cucumbers and gherkins are usually allowed to trail along the ground. Some training and trimmming is necessary to keep them within bounds. The plants should first be stopped after five or six leaves to encourage a branched habit. Large numbers of fruits are produced and the plants must be continually supplied with water and liquid fertilizer. Remember that both male and female flowers must be retained.

Use a mulch of black polythene to keep down weeds. As well as raising the soil temperature and helping to conserve moisture, the mulch also keeps the cucumber fruits off the soil, thus considerably reducing the likelihood of rotting.

Harvesting

Ridge cucumbers are shorter and fatter than the greenhouse types and are ready when 6-8 in long, from late July to late August onwards. Cut them as needed.

Gherkins should not be allowed to grow any longer than 3-4 in.

GHERKINS

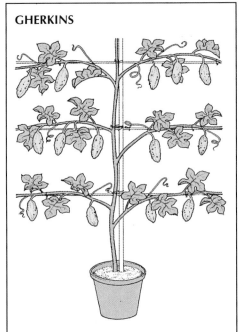

Gherkins are ideal for salads and for pickling. They can grow outside in the same way as ridge cucumbers, and can also be grown in 9 in pots and trained on to a cane and wire support. Sow two or three seeds in the centre of the pot and keep only the strongest seedling. Stop the plant after five or six leaves. Train the laterals along the support canes and retain all the flowers. Gherkins trained in this way make attractive potted plants for balconies or patios.

Ridge cucumbers

1 Early May to early June. Make holes 12 in wide and deep and fill them will organic manure. Replace the soil to produce mounds, 36 in apart each way.

2 Sow 3 seeds in each mount. Push the seeds ³/₄ in down into the soil. Cover each seed with a small jar.

3 When the seedlings have produced their first true leaves, thin to leave 1 plant at each mound.

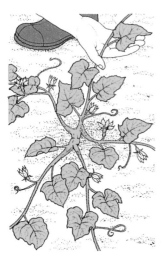

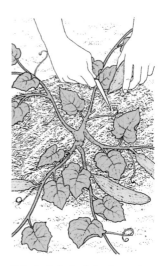

4 Stop the plants after 5-6 leaves and spread out the laterals so that they grow evenly around the main stems. Retain both male and female flowers.

5 Water and liquid feed the plants regularly. Mulch to conserve moisture and keep down weeds.

6 Late July to late August onwards. Cut ridge cucumbers as required with a sharp knife when they are 6-8 in long.

Marrows and squashes 1

MARROWS, SQUASHES, PUMPKINS AND COURGETTES

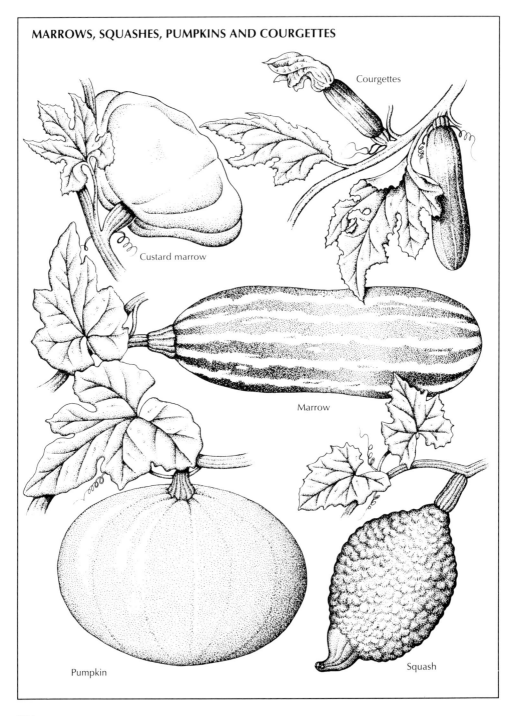

Courgettes

Custard marrow

Marrow

Pumpkin

Squash

Marrows, courgettes, pumpkins and squashes are closely related with only slight differences in growth habit, and both bush and trailing types are available. The fruits are quite different, however, and can be produced from June (early courgettes) until mid- to late September (pumpkins, squashes and marrows). Marrows and courgettes have similar fruits but courgettes are much smaller (about 6 in long). The skin colour varies from dark green, through stripes to golden yellow. Squashes have globular and spherical fruits with a colour range from yellow to green. Pumpkins produce large spherical fruits.

Soil and situation Well-drained soils are essential and these fruiting vegetables grow best in warm sunny positions.

Make planting holes which are a spade's width and depth. Fill the holes with well-rotted organic manure or garden compost and replace the soil to form a mound over each hole. All these vegetables grow vigorously and there is no need to add any fertilizer. Liquid feeding may be needed, however, especially when the fruits have set and are growing rapidly. Bush varieties should be spaced 36 in apart each way but trailing types must be spaced 5 ft apart.

Sowing For the most part these crops can be sown directly outside. However, it is often more convenient to raise the plants in pots and transplant later, and transplanting is essential for early courgette production under cloches. Sow 2-3 dry or a single "chitted" (see page 150) seed into 3 in peat or plastic pots filled with a proprietary potting compost such as John Innes No. 1. Push the seeds 3/4 in down into the compost. Keep them at a minimum temperature of 18°C/65°F and in good light to maintain sturdy growth. Allow 5-6 weeks to produce plants which have 3-4 true leaves at planting time. None of these vegetables, apart from the early cloched courgettes, must be planted out while a frost danger remains. Consequently, plants for early June planting should come from a mid-April sowing.

Direct sowing should take place in early to mid-May depending on the location. Sow 2-3 dry seeds or a single "chitted" seed into the top of each mound. Thin to one plant per mound when necessary.

Transplanting Transplant pot-grown plants into the tops of the prepared mounds when all danger of frost has passed. Put down a mulch around each plant while it is still small because it is difficult to get under the leaf canopy when the plants begin to grow rapidly. Keep the plants watered generously and liquid feed as required when the fruits begin to swell. Marrows and pumpkins being grown for exhibition need generous feeding.

Training Bush varieties of courgettes, marrows, pumpkins and squashes do not require stopping or training, but trailing varieties need attention. Each plant produces a number of lateral branches which should be stopped at 24 in. Fruiting laterals are then produced which bear male and female flowers. Both are needed and pollination usually takes place naturally with the aid of visiting insects. Early in the season or in cold weather it may be necessary to do some artificial pollinatino to ensure good fruit set. The female flowers have a small, undeveloped fruit immediately behind the large yellow flower. Male flowers are smaller and produce only pollen. Remove a male flower when pollen is being released and push it into a newly opened female flower.

Harvesting
These vegetables have a self-regulating mechanism which limits the number of fruits a plant carries. If fruits are grown for exhibition then the number per plant should be artificially limited. Marrows, pumpkins and squashes which mature in September should be kept off the soil to discourage slug attacks and rotting of the fruits. Mulching the plants helps or the developing fruits can be placed on sheets of glass or wood.

Regular cutting of courgettes ensures continuing production. Cut the fruits with a knife when they are 4-6 in long. Summer marrows are harvested as needed while those intended for winter use – along with pumpkins and squashes – should be cut in September before the frosts and stored in nets or on shelves in an airy, frost-free place.

Pests and diseases
Glasshouse whitefly may be a problem in warm, sunny seasons (see page 151).

Marrows and squashes 2

Preparing the mounds

1 Early to mid-May. Make planting holes which are a spade's width and depth, 5 ft apart each way for trailing varieties, 36 in for bush types.

2 Fill the holes with well-rotted manure or garden compost and replace the soil to form a mound over each hole. Water before sowing or planting.

3 Early to mid-May. Sow 2-3 seeds ¾ in deep in each mound. When each seedlings has 3-4 true leaves thin to leave 1 plant at each mound.

Transplanting

Training trailing plants

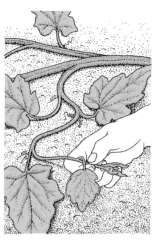

4 Early to mid-May. Transplant pot-grown, previously watered, plants into the tops of the mounds when all danger of frost has passed and mulch.

5 Mid-May onwards. Keep the plants well watered and liquid feed regularly when the fruits begin to swell.

6 June. Pinch out the growing points on the plant's lateral branches when they are 24 in long and train them evenly around each plant.

EARLY COURGETTES UNDER CLOCHES

Sow the seed in the normal way but aim to transplant the young courgettes in early May. This means sowing must take place in mid-March. Prepare planting holes as for outdoor crops but cover the row of mounds with glass cloches or polythene tunnels to warm up the soil before planting. Then remove the cloches in order to completely cover the row of mounds with black polythene, which is dug in at the sides to bury the edges.

Slit the polythene over each mound and thoroughly water each planting position before setting out the previously watered plants. Cover with cloches immediately after planting. If the soil is well soaked before planting further waterings should not be necessary. Ventilate freely on warm, sunny days. This also allows pollinating insects to do their work. Remove the cloches when the plants reach the glass and frost danger has passed.

Pollination

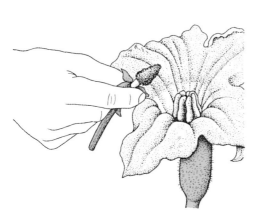

7 In cold conditions early in the season hand-pollinate by pushing a pollen-releasing male flower into a newly-opened female flower.

Harvesting

8 September. Place the maturing fruits on sheets of wood to discourage slug and fungal attacks and cut as required, but before frosts occur.

Sweet peppers

Sweet peppers are in the same family as tomatoes and potatoes. They are grown for their large fruits, which are usually harvested green although they can be left on the plant until they turn red.

Cultivation
Sweet peppers need similar growing conditions to tomatoes, although higher temperature and humidity is necessary. They grow best in greenhouses but it may be possible to grow them outside in mild sheltered areas or even in less favourable locations with the aid of cloches or tall-sided cold frames.

Soil and situation When grown outside, peppers must have well-drained, fertile soil. They need an easy-to-drain, sunny and sheltered site. They also require large amounts of moisture and the soil should be improved with well-rotted manure or garden compost during winter digging.

In greenhouses sweet peppers may be grown in the soil, in pots or in growing bags.

Open ground crops should receive a base dressing of 1-2 oz per square yard of a balanced general fertilizer before planting and must be liquid fed regularly once the fruits begin to swell. Bag- and pot-grown plants require liquid feeding from an earlier stage and need very careful watering.

Plant raising High temperatures are needed to grow sweet pepper plants satisfactorily and, even then, it takes 10-12 weeks from seed sowing until planting. A temperature of 21°C/70°F is needed for seed germination, reducing to 18°C/65°F for the remainder of the plant-raising period. Sow the seed thinly in compost in a seed tray or pan and cover with a thin layer of compost. Water and cover with a sheet of glass and a piece of newspaper. Turn the glass daily to prevent condensation dripping on to the seedlings.

As soon as the seedlings are large enough

Greenhouse planting

1 March onwards. Sow the seed thinly on moistened compost. Cover with ⅛ in of compost then glass and newspaper. Turn glass daily. Keep at 21°C/70°F until growing well.

2 As soon as the seedlings are large enough to handle prick single seeds into 3 in peat pots. Feed to maintain growth.

3 Mid-May onwards. (heated greenhouse) or 10-12 weeks after sowing, put single plants in 9 in pots, spaced 18 in apart each way. Water and liquid feed regularly.

to handle, prick them out into individual 3 in peat or plastic pots containing a proprietary potting compost such as John Innes No. 1. Liquid feed to maintain growth. Alternatively, buy plants from a nursery.

Greenhouse planting Sweet peppers can be planted in heated greenhouses (15°-18°C/60°-65°F) from March onwards but delay planting in unheated structures until mid-May. Plant three plants in each standard-sized growing bag or space individual plants in 9 in pots 18 in apart in each direction.

Planting outside Plant outdoor sweet peppers 18 in apart each way in mid-June and give initial protection with cloches.

Training Sweet peppers have a bushy habit and they are encouraged to branch if the growing point is removed when the plants are about 6 in high. Support and tie them to bamboo canes if necessary. Cold glass and outside plants grow only 24 in high but heated greenhouse peppers may be taller.

Harvesting
From July onwards peppers in the greenhouse can be harvested; those grown outdoors will not be ready until late August or September. Cut the fruits as required. Green fruits on greenhouse or protected pepper plants turn red if left on the plant for a further two or three weeks.

Pests and diseases
Treat aphids, whitefly or red spider mite on sight as described on pages 31-33.

Diseases are not common on sweet peppers but grey-brown sunken areas may appear on the fruits when the plants have been grown without sufficient water. The sunken areas go soft and may become colonized by grey mould (*Botrytis cinerea*) (see page 29). Always keep peppers well supplied with water, especially in isolated growing systems such as pots or growing bags.

4 When the plants are 6 in tall remove the growing point on each, leaving 3-4 branches. Support the plants with canes if necessary.

5 Throughout the growing season spray aphids, whitefly or red spider mite on sight with a suitable insecticide, or use biological control.

6 July onwards (August onwards outside). Cut the green fruits as required. Leave in the greenhouse or under protection for a further 2-3 weeks if red fruits are desired.

Aubergines

The aubergine is a sub-tropical plant grown for its egg-shaped fruits which give rise to the common name of "egg-plant". The fruits are usually purple, but white-fruited types are also available.

Cultivation

Aubergines have similar requirements to tomatoes and sweet peppers. They grow best in warm, sunny, humid conditions and are most successful in greenhouses, although they can be grown outside, especially if cloches and polythene shelters are used.

Soil and situation Outside crops must be grown in well-drained fertile soils and in a sunny, sheltered part of the garden. They should be given 1-2 oz per square yard of a general, balanced fertilizer before planting and should be liquid fed regularly after the fruits being to swell.

Plant raising The plant raising procedure is similar to that for sweet peppers (see page 158) and, again, high temperatures are necessary. In early March sow the seed thinly in seed trays or pans and keep them at a temperature of 21°C/70°F. Germination is slow and seedling growth also requires high temperatures. Prick out the seedlings into individual 3 in peat or plastic pots as soon as they can be handled. Maintain the temperature at 18°-21°C/65°-70°F and begin liquid feeding if plant growth slows down. Allow at least 10-12 weeks from seed sowing to planting.

Alternatively, purchase the plants from a nursery or garden centre.

Planting outside Do not plant aubergines outside until all danger of frost has passed and the soil has begun to warm up; early June is soon enough. Cover the soil with cloches for 2-3 weeks before planting and then put them back over the aubergines to encourage establishment. Keep the cloches in place until the plants reach the glass.

If cloches are not available, erect a clear polythene screen around the plants to provide shelter and warmth. Space aubergine plants 24 in apart each way outdoors.

Greenhouse planting Greenhouse aubergines can be planted earlier, from April onwards if heating is available. Plant them in individual 9 in pots or in growing bags with two plants per bag. If using pots fill them with a proprietary potting compost, such as John Innes No. 1, and in either case liquid feed the plants at every watering. Best results are obtained if the temperature can be maintained at 15°-18°C/60°-65°F. Do not plant in an unheated greenhouse until early May.

Training Remove the growing point of each plant when 9-12 in high to encourage a branched habit. Aubergines are less bushy than sweet peppers and only 3-4 branches should be allowed per plant. Space out and support the branches with string attached to overhead wires or bamboo canes.

Regular feeding and watering is necessary but "little-and-often" is the best policy to avoid the danger of waterlogging or drying out. Fruits develop readily in warm, sunny weather but good-sized aubergines are formed only if the number per plant is restricted to five or six. Remove any other flowers which then appear.

Harvesting

From late August to September, depending on the variety, cut aubergines with a sharp knife when they reach 6-8 in length and have turned to a rich purple.

Pests and diseases

Aphids, whitefly and red spider mite can be particularly troublesome on aubergines. Treat as described on pages 31-33.

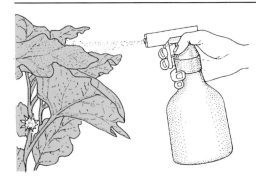

5 Throughout summer. Water sparingly but very regularly and liquid feed at the same time. Spray against aphids, whitefly and red spider mite if they occur.

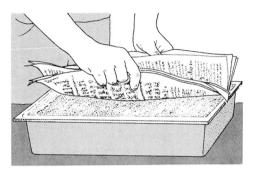

1 Early March. Sow the seed on moistened seed compost. cover with ⅛ in of compost, then with glass and newspaper. Keep at 21°C/70°F and turn the glass daily.

2 As soon as they are large enough to handle, prick out the seedlings singly into 3 in peat pots. Keep at 18°-21°C/65°-70°F. If growth slows down, water and feed.

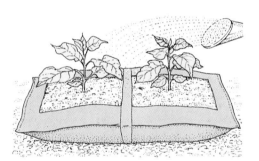

3 April to May (June outdoors). Plant 2 previously watered aubergine plants in a growing bag and water. For best results keep temperature at 15°-18°C/60°-65°F.

4 Pinch out the growing points when the plants are 9-12 in high, to encourage the growth of 3-4 strong branches. Support the plants with canes.

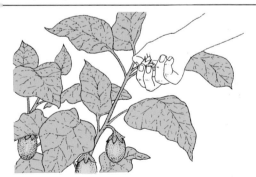

6 Remove all but 5-6 developing fruits on each plant, keeping them evenly spaced, and pinch out any extra flowers that form.

7 Late August onwards (depending on the variety). When the fruits are 6-8 in long and a rich purple colour, cut them off with a sharp knife.

Mushrooms

The cultivated mushroom, which is commonly grown by commercial producers and less often by gardeners in Europe, is a close relative of the edible wild mushroom *Agaricus campestris*. The condition, quality and sterility of the compost on which the mushroom fungus is grown hold the key to successful mushroom cultivation, and it is extremely difficult for home gardeners to produce reliably uniform compost. A brief outline of all the stages in mushroom growing is given here, but more certain results are obtained by purchasing the proprietary bags, boxes or tubs of mushroom compost which have already been spawned. These containers must be kept in a suitable place at the recommended temperature and watered carefully to produce mushrooms.

Compost making

Wheat straw from stables is the ideal material from which to prepare mushroom compost. It contains sufficient manure to cause it to ferment, give off ammonia and break down, but the straw must be watered and turned regularly at four or five day intervals. Dry straw can be used but then an artificial activator must also be added to initiate the breakdown processes. The compost may become greasy, although this can be avoided by mixing at least 1 lb of gypsum with each hundredweight of straw. During composting the straw should change into a dark brown friable material without any smell of ammonia. The compost should be open textured and spongy, but hold only a little water rather than be waterlogged.

Commercial composting takes nearly two weeks and is followed by a week of peak heating when the compost is kept at a high temperature (60°C/140°F), to ensure that straw breakdown is complete and all harmful micro-organisms are killed. The home gardener can seldom peak heat this material, so must continue the composting process until the compost has the correct colour, consistency and smell. It may take 3-4 weeks.

Spawning

The compost is then put into boxes, buckets or bags prior to spawning. Do not spawn the compost until the temperature in the middle of the container has fallen below 24°C/75°F. The propagation material for mushrooms is cereal grains or manure on which the fungus has been grown. The grains or manure are covered with a whitish fungal growth and are called "spawn". Put 9-12 in of compost

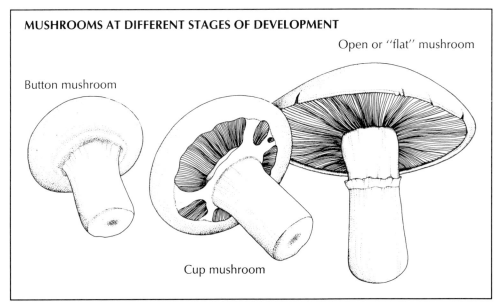

MUSHROOMS AT DIFFERENT STAGES OF DEVELOPMENT

Open or "flat" mushroom

Button mushroom

Cup mushroom

in the container and lightly firm it down. Break manure spawn into golf-ball sized pieces and push them 1 in down into the compost at 10-12 in spacings each way. Sprinkle grain spawn on to the compost surface and mix it into the top 2 in. Keep the containers in a warm, dark place until the mushroom fungus begins to grow ("run"). this takes 7-10 days.

Casing
Mushrooms are produced directly on the compost surface but a covering layer (casing) is usually put on to the compost when spawn running has begun. The casing retains moisture and prevents the compost surface drying out; it also helps to supply water evenly to the developing mushrooms. A mixture of equal parts peat and lump chalk is the best casing material, and it should be thoroughly moistened before application. Put a 2 in layer over the compost.

Growing
Keep the containers at 16°-18°C/60°-65°F in a reasonably humid atmosphere. Very dry conditions cause the compost and casing to dry out, whereas prolonged dampness causes the fungus and developing mushrooms to rot.

Water carefully, giving small quantities at regular intervals rather than heavy doses irregularly. The first pin-head mushrooms should appear about three weeks after casing but it takes another 7-10 days before they are ready to harvest. At lower temperatures the mushrooms grow and fruit more slowly. After the first flush of mushrooms has been harvested there is a delay of 1-2 weeks before the next flush appears. Each crop of mushrooms produces several flushes over a 6-8 week period.

Harvesting
Twist the mushrooms off when they have reached the required stage of development. Tightly rounded button mushrooms are popular today, but the open "flats" – similar to those found in the wild during early autumn – have much more flavour. Use a sharp knife to trim off the surface of the cropping bed to remove all broken stalks and debris. Fill in any holes left from harvesting with additional casing material. After the final flush of mushrooms has been picked the compost should be emptied out and used as an organic manure in the garden. Never re-use mushroom compost because it is likely to contain harmful pests and diseases.

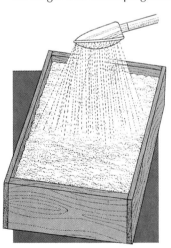

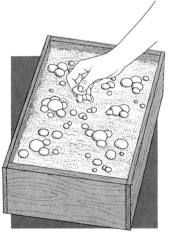

1 Water mushrooms regularly but lightly. Use the fine rose of a watering can to apply water.

2 Twist mushrooms away from the surface of the bed and remove any broken or damaged stalks.

3 Re-fill the holes left by removed mushrooms with casing material to ensure longer productivity.

Okra

Okra, also known as ladies' fingers and gumbo, is closely related to the garden *Hibiscus* and is grown for its long, green, finger-shaped, edible pods.

Cultivation

Okra is naturally a tropical plant, and so in temperate regions it grows best in a greenhouse or under polythene tunnels, although it may occasionally be possible to grow it outside in warm, sheltered areas that have long, hot summers.

Soil and situation When grown outside, okra needs a rich, loamy soil and a very sunny site sheltered from wind. If necessary, improve the soil by incorporating well-rooted manure during winter digging. In a greenhouse, okra may be grown in beds or pots.

Both protected outdoor crops and those in greenhouses require regular watering during the growing season.

Plant raising Fairly high temperatures are necessary to grow okra satisfactorily. A temperature of 18°-21°C/65°-70°F is necessary for seed germination and the remainder of the plant-raising period. Sow the seed thinly on compost in a seed tray or pan, or singly in peat pots. Cover with a thin layer of compost and then water. Then cover with a sheet of glass and a piece of newspaper. Turn the glass daily to prevent condensation dripping on to the developing seedlings. Germination takes place in 7-25 days, depending on the temperature.

As soon as the seedlings are large enough to handle, prick them out into 3 in peat or

Greenhouse planting

1 February onwards. Sow the seed on moist compost. Cover with ⅛ in of compost, then glass and newspaper. Turn the glass daily. Keep at 18°-21°C/65°-70°F.

2 As soon as the seedlings are large enough to handle, prick them out singly into 3 in peat or plastic pots filled with proprietary potting compost.

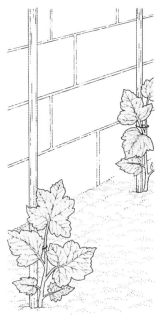

3 March onwards (heated greenhouse). As soon as the roots of the seedlings fill the pots, transplant them to 10 in pots or plant in a bed, spaced 21-24 in apart each way. Support with canes.

plastic pots containing potting compost.

Greenhouse planting Okra can be planted in a heated greenhouse in early spring, but delay planting in unheated structures until mid-May. Plant individual plants in 10 in pots or space them 21-24 in apart in each direction in a greenhouse bed. Before planting, insert supporting stakes. In the greenhouse and out-doors it is usually necessary to pinch out the plants' growing points when they are 9-12 in high. This encourages bushy plants to pro-duce a succession of young growth and hence flowers and fruit.

Planting outside Plant outdoor okra 21-24 in apart each way in early June. Before planting insert supporting stakes and warm up the ground with polythene tunnels. Again, stop the plants when they are about 9-12 in tall.

From time to time, tie in the plants to the supporting stakes.

Harvesting

The pods are ready for harvesting when they are young and tender and the seeds are still soft. Pick okra in the greenhouse from June onwards and those grown outdoors from September. Cut off the immature pods with scissors regularly to ensure a succession of new pods over aperiod of several weeks. Do not allow the pods to mature because odl pods are unpalatable.

Pests and diseases

Glasshouse whitefly, aphids and red spider mites may cause problems (see pages 31-33).

Planting outdoors

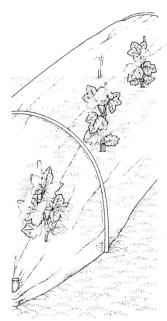

4 Early June. As soon as the roots of the seedlings fill the pots, plant them out spaced 21-24 in apart each way. Stake each plant and cover with polythene tunnels.

5 When the plants (greenhouse and under cloches) are 9-12 in high pinch out the growing points to encourage a bushy habit and a succession of fruits.

6 June onwards (September onwards outside). Cut the young, tender pods regularly for a succession of new pods over several weeks.

Florence fennel

Florence fennel is grown for its bulb-like swollen leaf bases which taste of aniseed. The green-white "bulbs" can be sliced and used raw in salads or they can be cooked whole in boiling water and served with a white or cheese sauce.

The feathery leaves can be used for flavouring as a substitute for *Foeniculum vulgare* or common fennel (see page 179), of which Florence fennel is a subspecies.

Cultivation

Florence fennel is grown widely in Italy because it thrives in the warm Mediterranean climate, but it is possible to grow the plant in cool temperate regions. Careful plant raising is required, however, and good-sized basal stems are produced only in warm, sunny summers.

Soil and situation The plant grows best in well-drained, warm soils which permit early

Sowing in the greenhouse

1 April to July. Sow successive batches of seed thinly in a seed tray and keep at a temperature of 16°C/60°F.

Pricking out

2 As soon as they can be handled prick the seedlings out singly into individual 3 in peat pots. Keep at 13°C/55°F, well-ventilated, and in good light.

Blanching

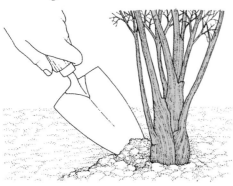

4 When the plant bases have swollen to the size of a golf ball blanch by drawing up soil around the lower parts of each stem. Continue earthing up for 4 weeks.

5 Alternatively, blanch Florence fennel by tying cardboard collars around the base of each plant.

sowing or planting. Well-rotted manure or compost should be incorporated during winter digging to retain moisture and encourage the leaf bases to swell. They must swell with no obstructions, so avoid stony soils. Heavy clay soils are not suitable for this vegetable. The leaf bases are blanched at the end of the season by drawing soil up around them and the soil must be easily cultivated for this purpose. Rapid growth is encouraged by

Transplanting

3 Four weeks later. Rake in 1-2 oz per square yard of fertilizer and transplant the seedlings at 9-12 in intervals in rows 18 in apart. Hoe and water regularly.

Harvesting

6 Late June to late September. Four weeks after the start of blanching, when the basal stems are the size of a tennis ball, cut beneath them with a sharp knife.

incorporating 1-2 oz per square yard of a balanced general fertilizer, such as Growmore, before sowing or planting.

Sowing Florence fennel can be sown directly outside from April onwards, although germination can be slow and growth is often poor. If it is sown, use $1/2$ in deep drills which are 18 in apart. Sow thinly and thin the seedlings to 9-12 in apart as soon as possible. Do not sow too early because the plants run immediately to flower if there is too much cold weather at the seedling stage.

Alternatively, the plants can be transplanted after raising in a slightly heated greenhouse. Sow the seed thinly in a seed tray or pan and germinate at a temperature of 16aC/60°F. Prick the seedlings out into small, individual peat pots as soon as they can be handled. Reduce the temperature to 13°C/55°F and grow in good light with plenty of ventilation in order to produce strong, sturdy plants.

Greenhouse sowings can be made from April until July and the plants should be ready for transplanting in about four weeks. Plant them at 9-12 in intervals in rows which are 18 in apart.

Blanching

Hoe the plants carefully to keep down weeds and keep them well watered at all times. Plants grown in dry conditions do not produce good-sized "bulbs". When the leaf bases begin to swell it is time to blanch them. Draw soil around the small bulbs when they reach the size of a golf-ball and continue the process through the summer.

Florence fennel can also be blanched by tying cardboard collars around the bases of individual plants.

Harvesting

Harvesting can begin about four weeks from the start of earthing up, by which time the "bulbs" should be slightly larger than a tennis ball. Harvest the entire leaf bases by cutting beneath them with a sharp knife.

Pests and diseases

Florence fennel is generally free of pest and disease trouble but it may be necessary to take precautions against slugs (see page 33).

Hamburg parsley/Horseradish

Hamburg parsley is in the carrot and parsnip family and it is a valuable, if neglected, winter vegetable. It has parsley-flavoured leaves and parsnip-like roots which have a mild flavour of celery.

Cultivation

It is a hardy plant and must be sown early in the year to develop good-sized roots.

Sowing Sow the seed in ½ in deep drills which are 12 in apart as early in the year as soil and weather conditions allow. Mid-March is an ideal time in continental Europe, where the vegetable is more widely grown than it is in Great Britain. Germination is slow and it is important to keep down weeds during the seedling stages. Hoe carefully around the plants, taking care not to damage the developing tap roots.

Thin the seedlings to 9 in apart as soon as they are large enough to handle. Water generously throughout the summer and top-dress with a nitrogenous fertilizer, such as nitro-chalk, at 1-2 oz per square yard to maintain good growth.

As with celeriac, the roots continue to grow well into autumn and the largest roots come from the longest growing season.

Harvesting

Lift the roots as soon as they are needed from November onwards. They are frost hardy but it is worth strawing them over in very severe winters.

Hamburg parsley

1 Late March. Sow the seed in ½ in deep drills which are 12 in apart. Keep down weeds by hoeing very carefully.

2 As soon as the seedlings are large enough to handle, thin them until they are 9 in apart.

Horseradish

1 December. Remove pencil-thickness roots from established plants and cut them into 6-8 in lengths.

2 March. With the thick ends uppermost, plant the roots at an angle of 45° in dibber-made holes.